The Infinite Imagination

Adult Coloring Book Vol.2

About The Artist

I grew up in an artistic family and have been an artist ever since I was a little girl.

At 17 years old I had my first professional art gallery exhibit. Later, I studied Architecture and Interior design, with my specialty being furniture and lighting design.

Over the years I have created hundreds of paintings and designed many products, such as, dog toys and clothes, furniture and a skin care/cosmetic line.

"I believe art transforms our emotions and opens our visual awareness".

Bereniche Aguiar

Art and Shop Website: www.berenicheaguiar.com

Recommendations

I recommend only using colored pencils to prevent any color bleed through on the pages. I also suggest putting a piece of cardboard underneath the page being colored, for more support, if it is desired to press hard with the colored pencils.

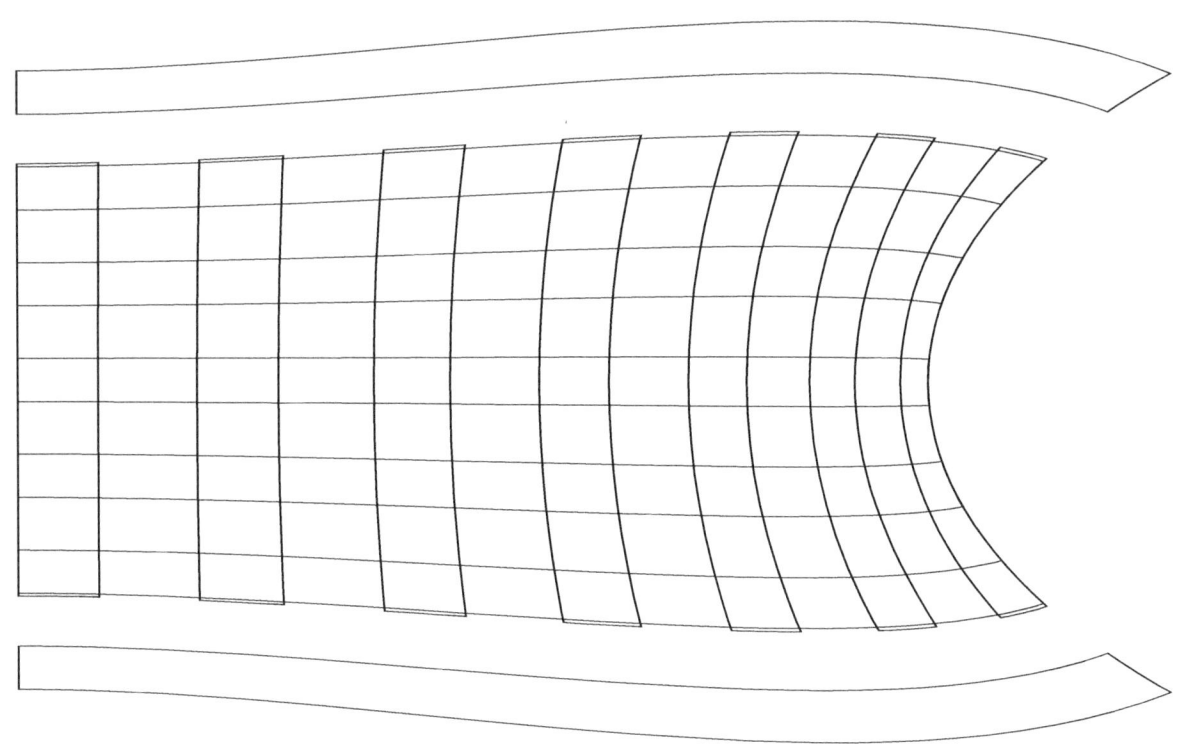

The full size drawing is on page 34

D# 2050

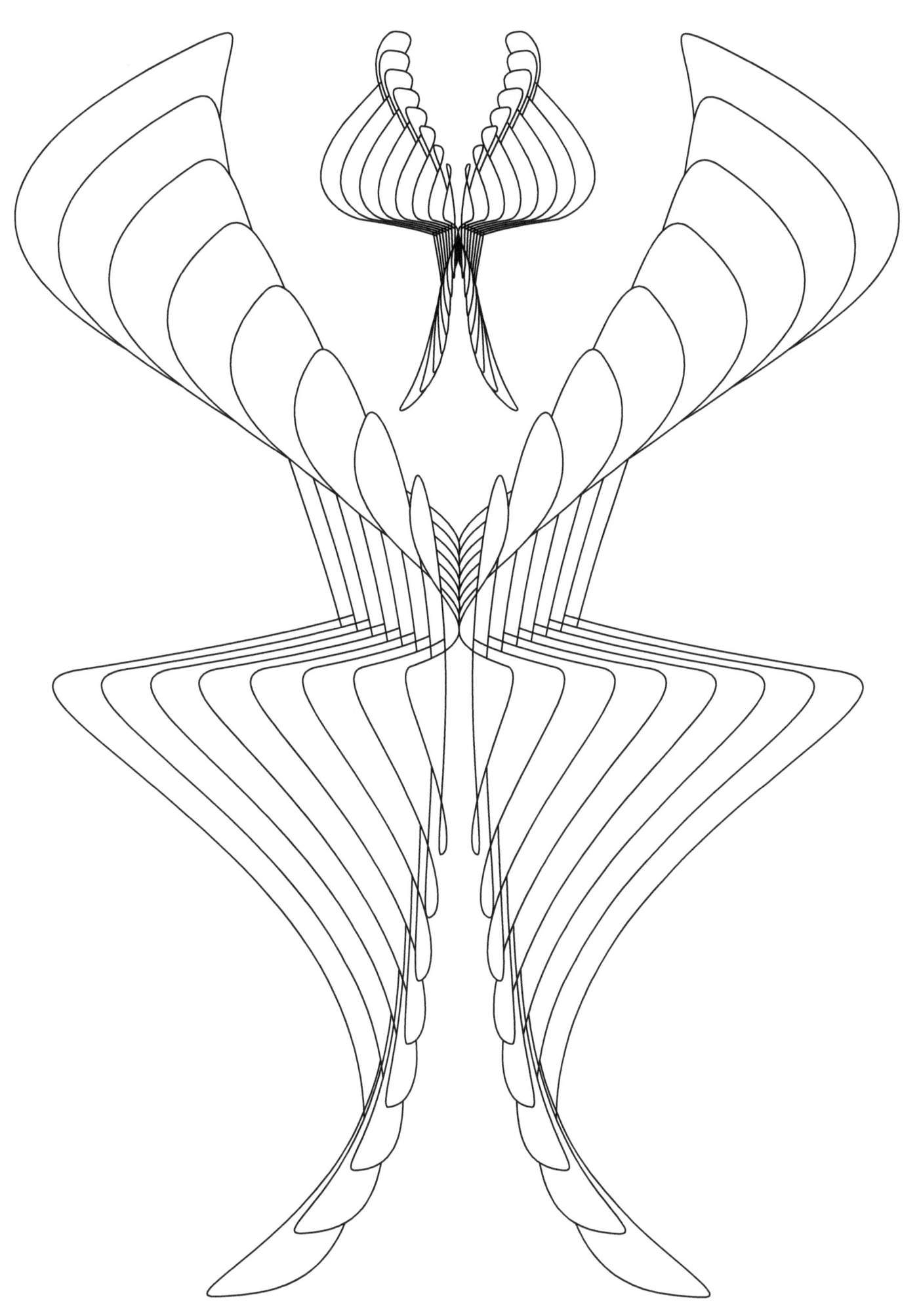

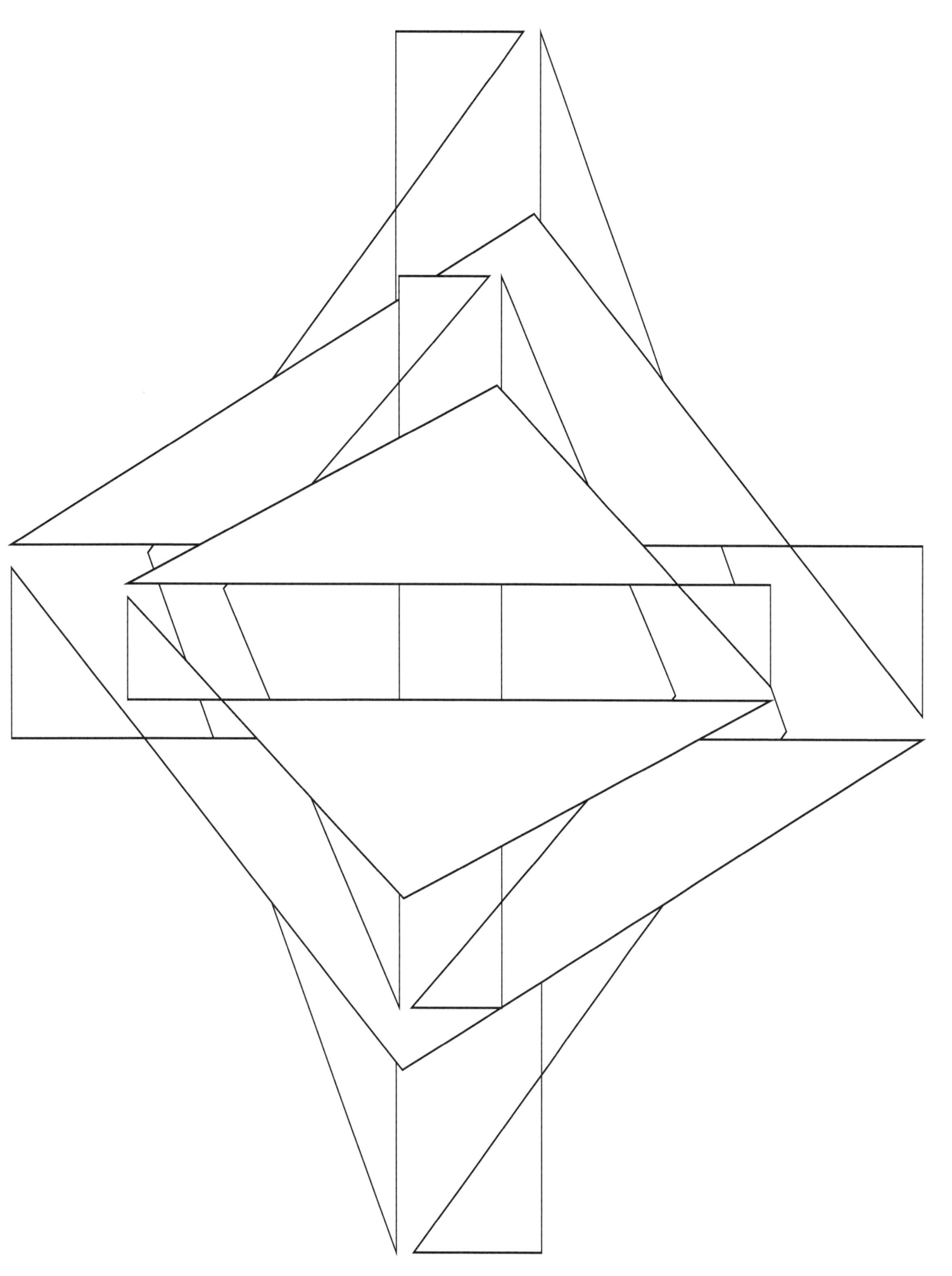

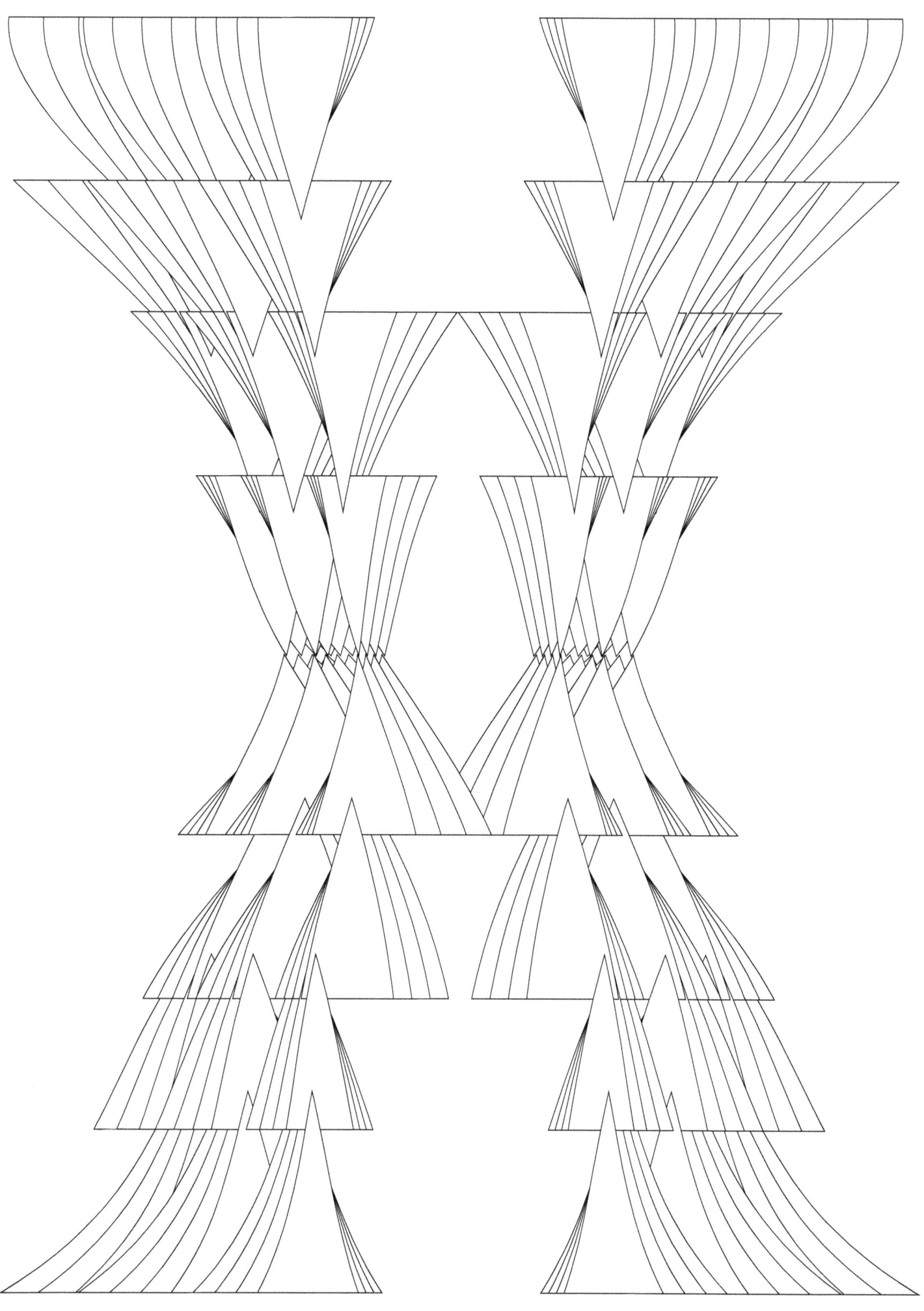

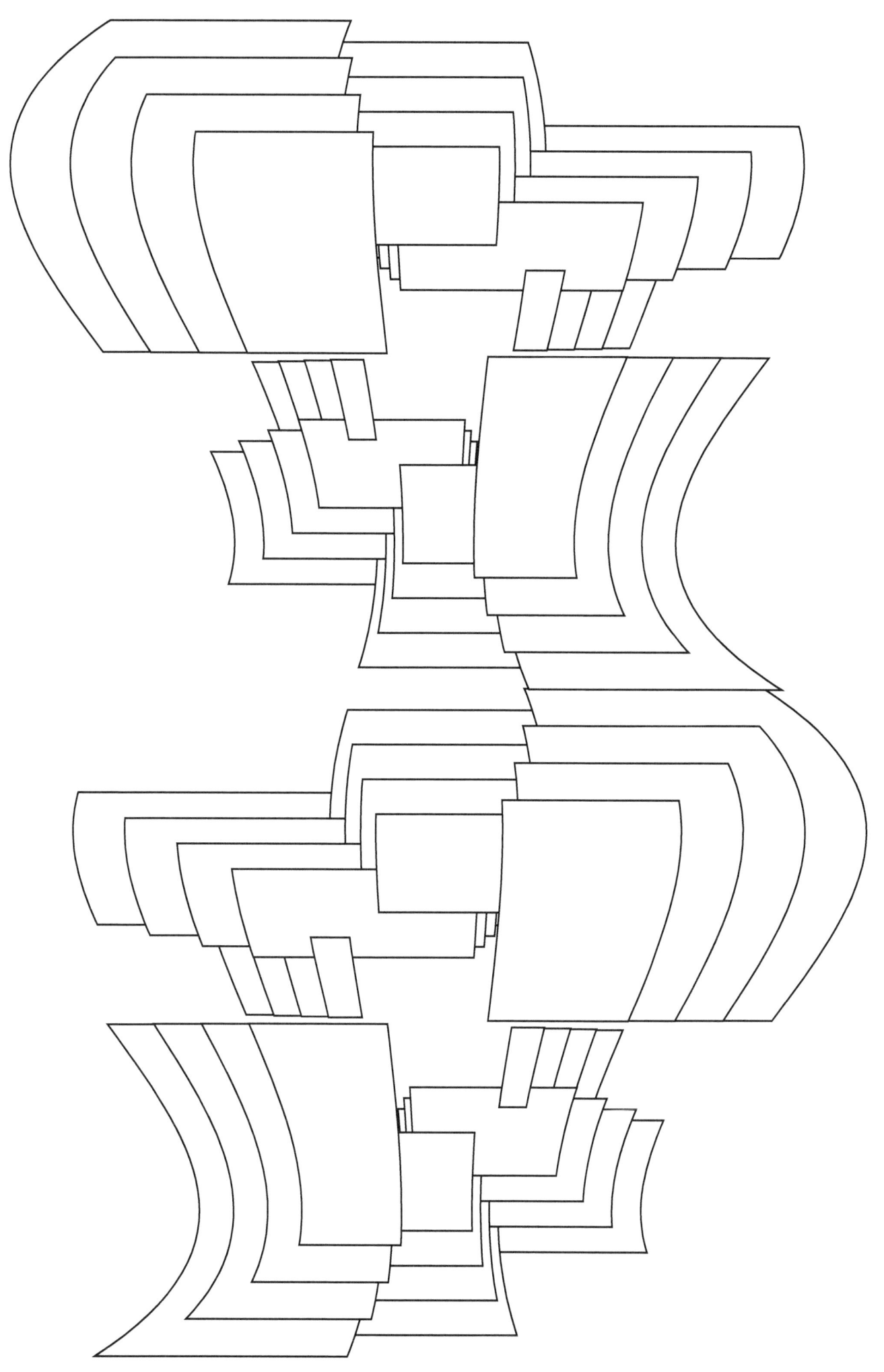

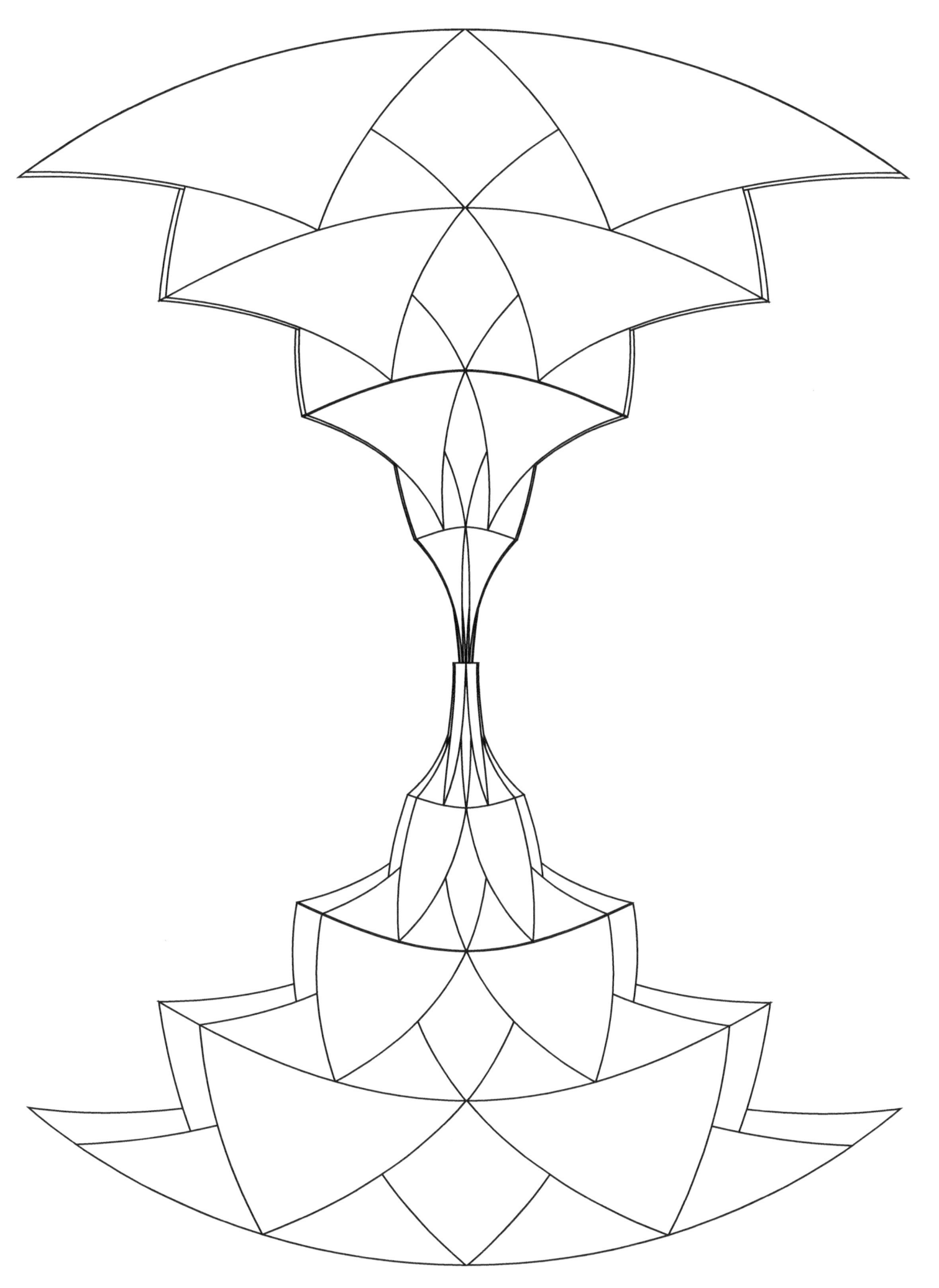

D# 1830

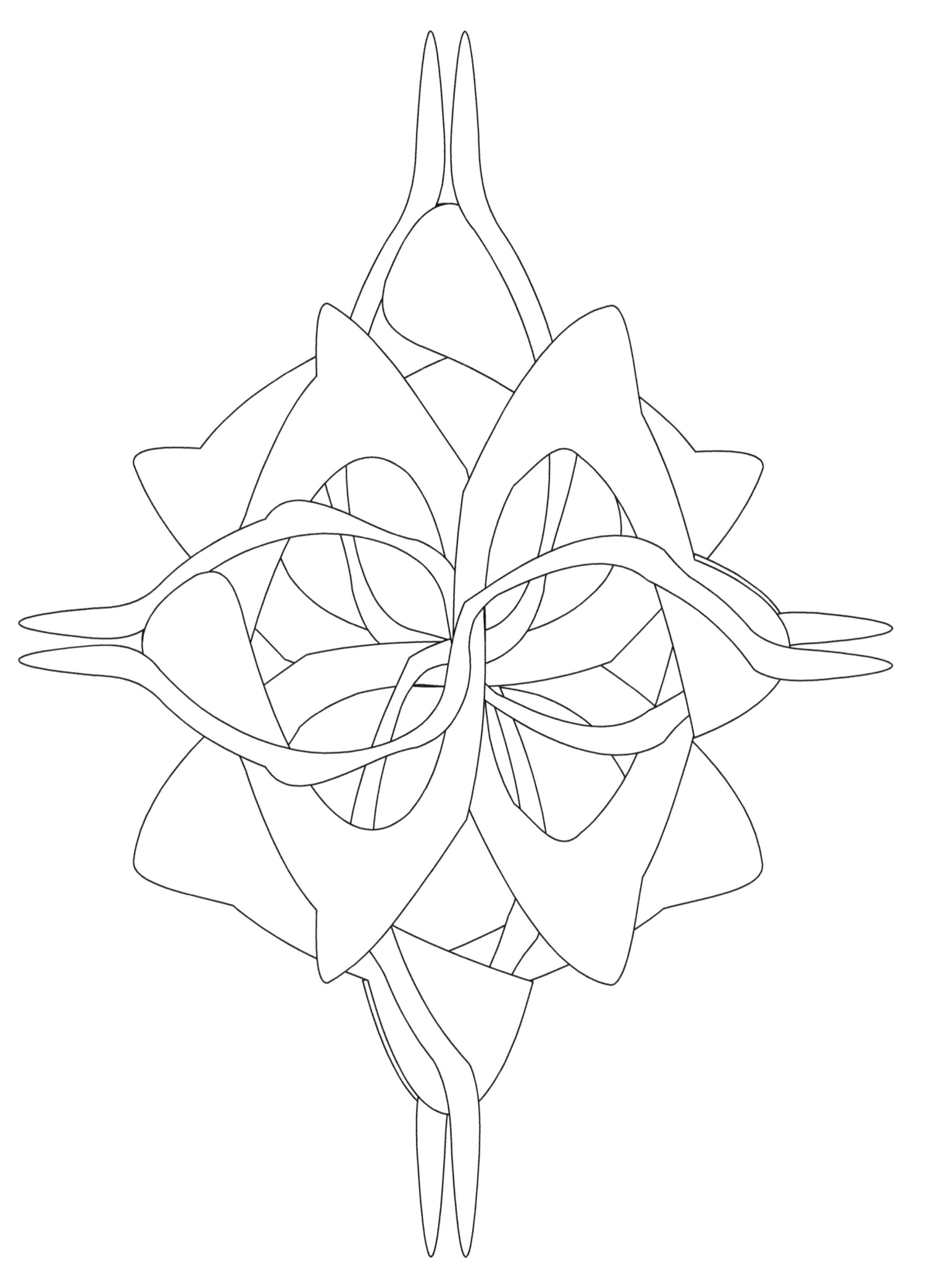

D# 1937

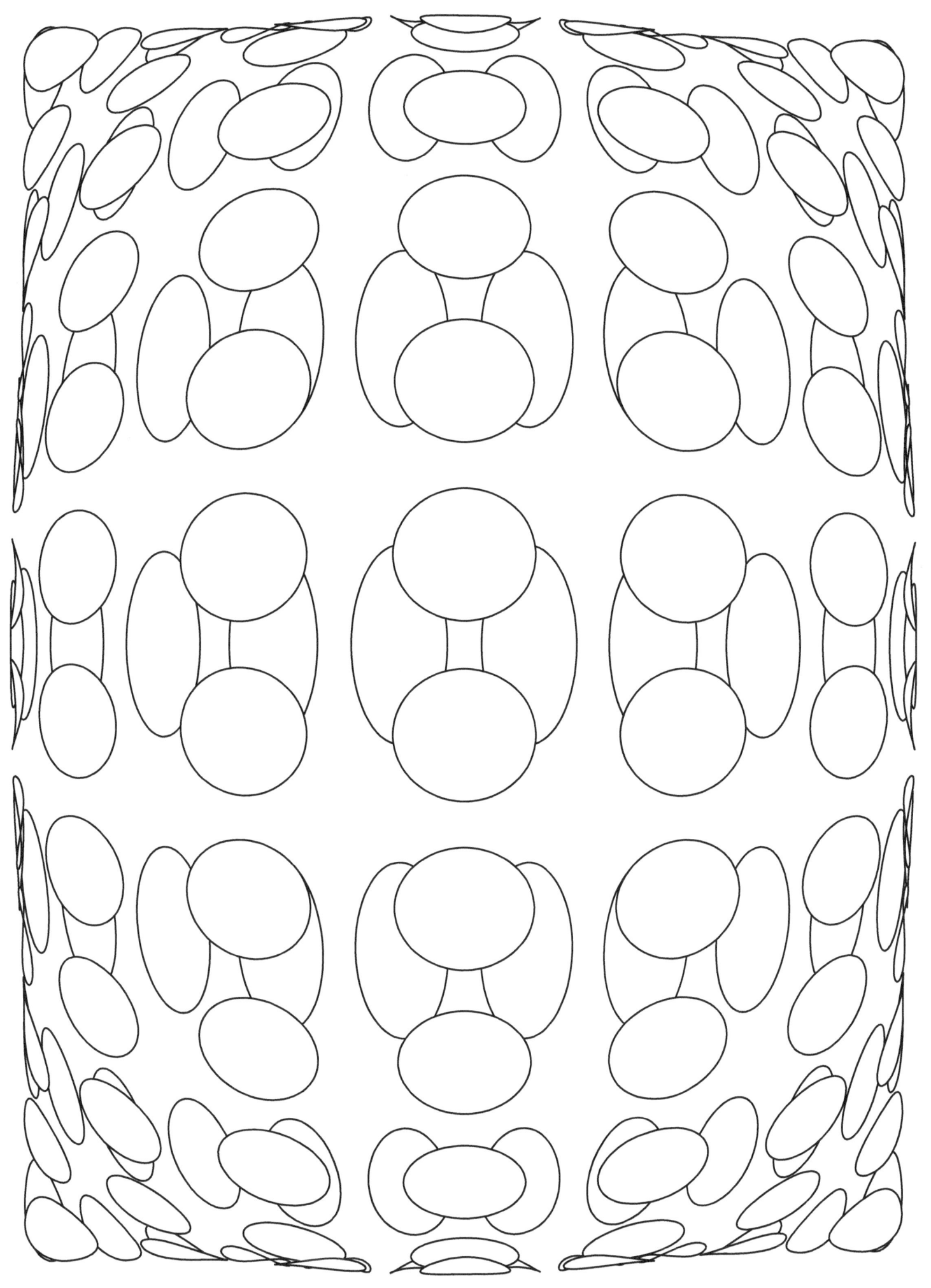

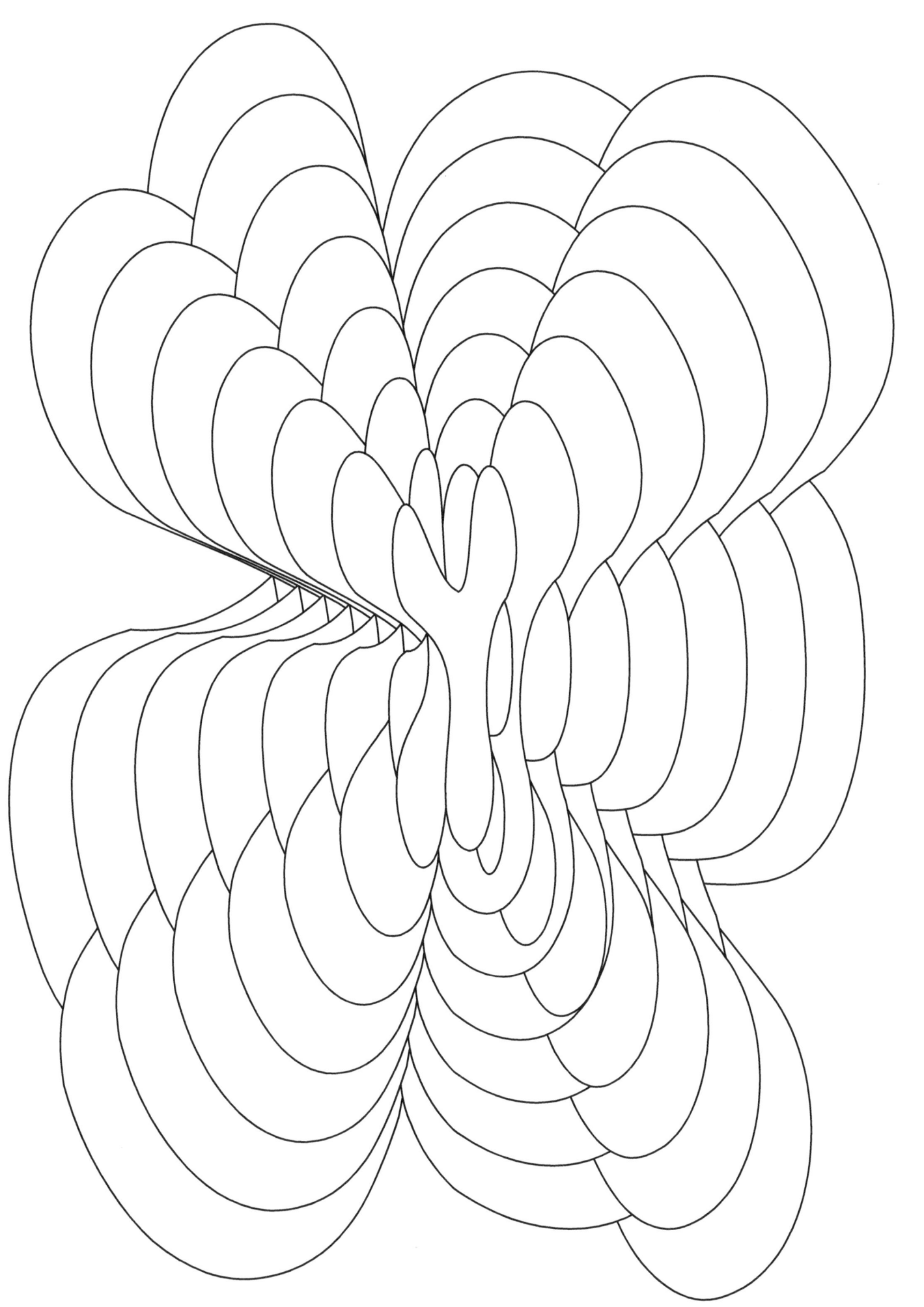

D# 1963

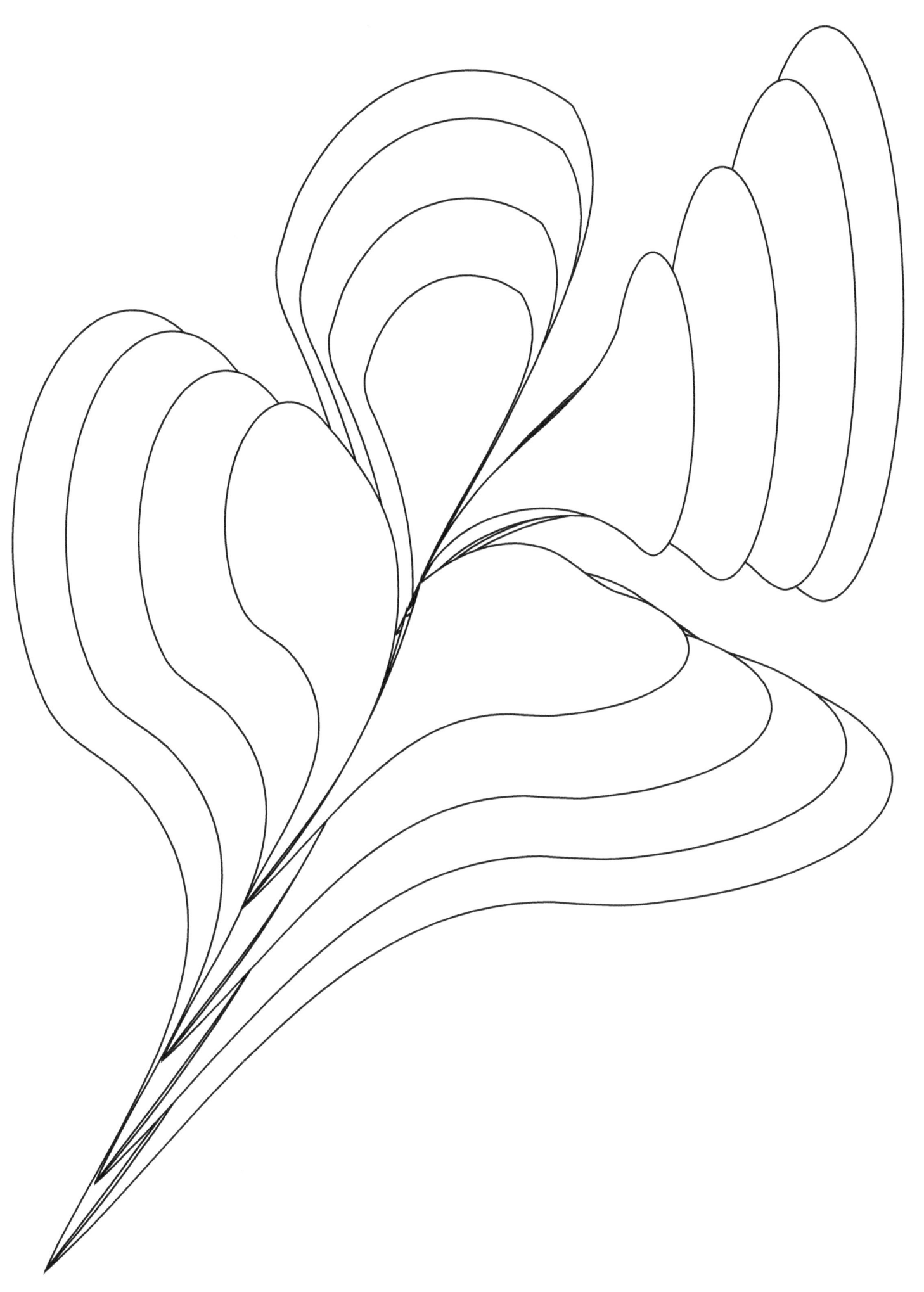

D# 2055

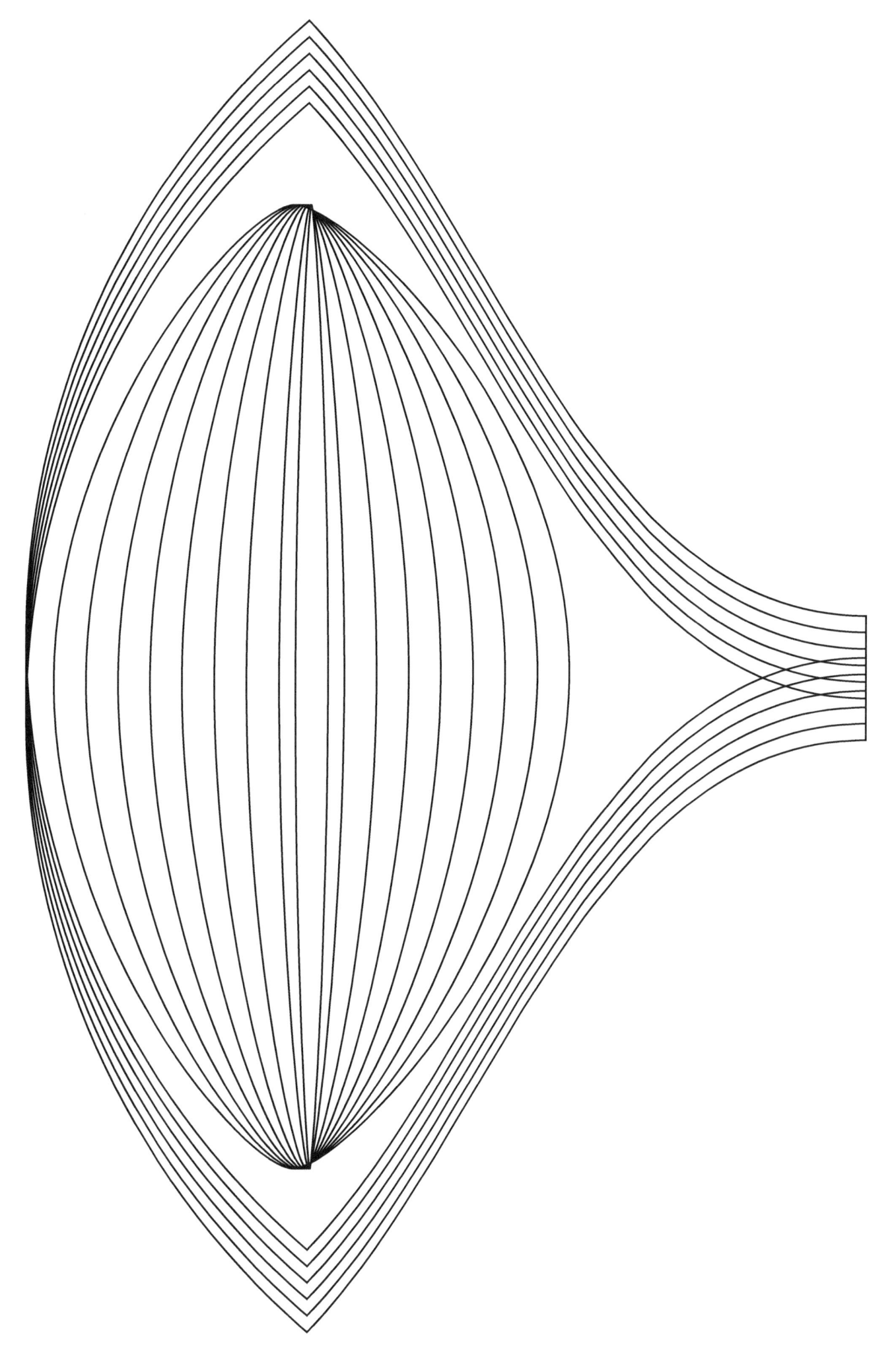

D# 2052

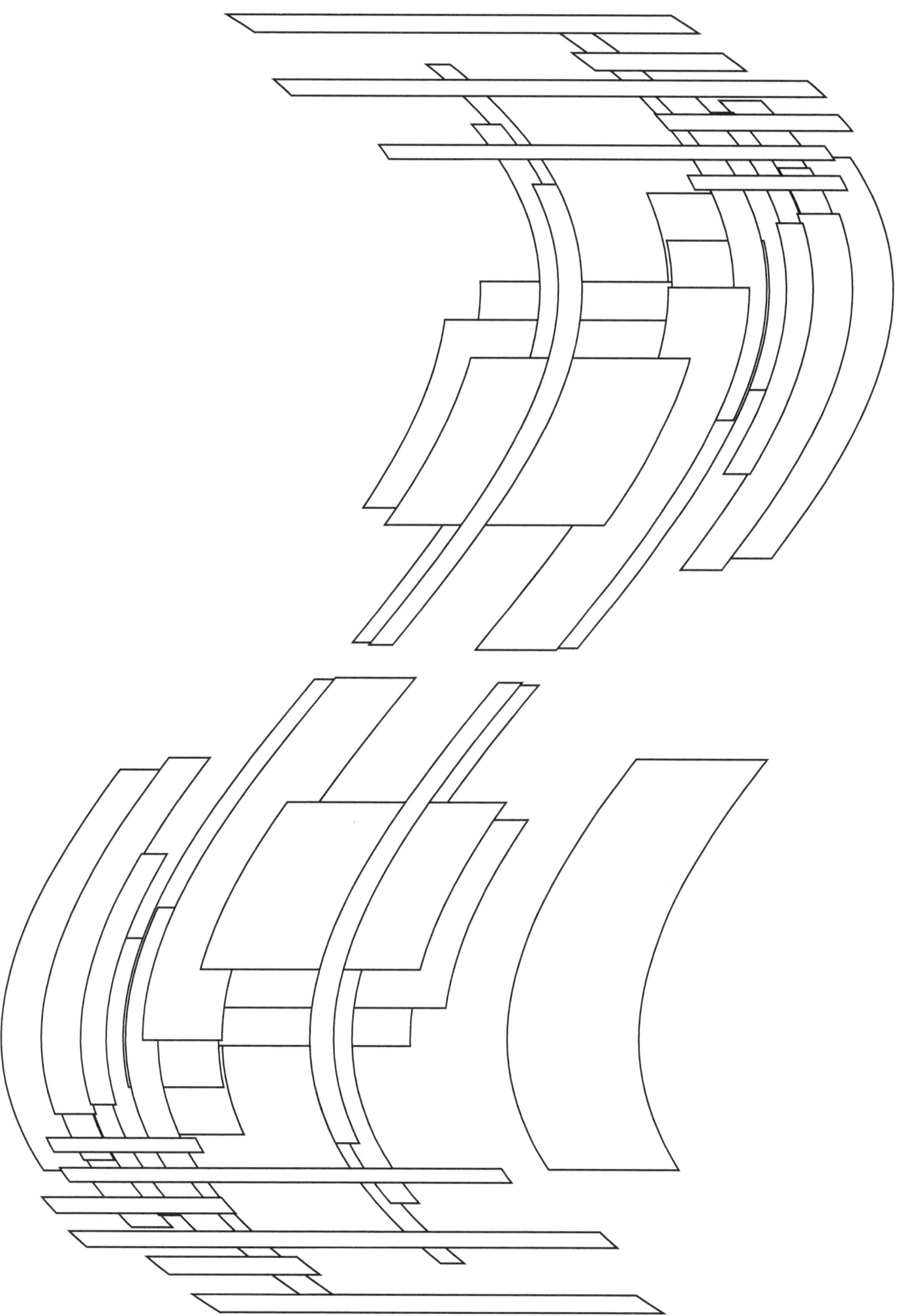

D# 2136

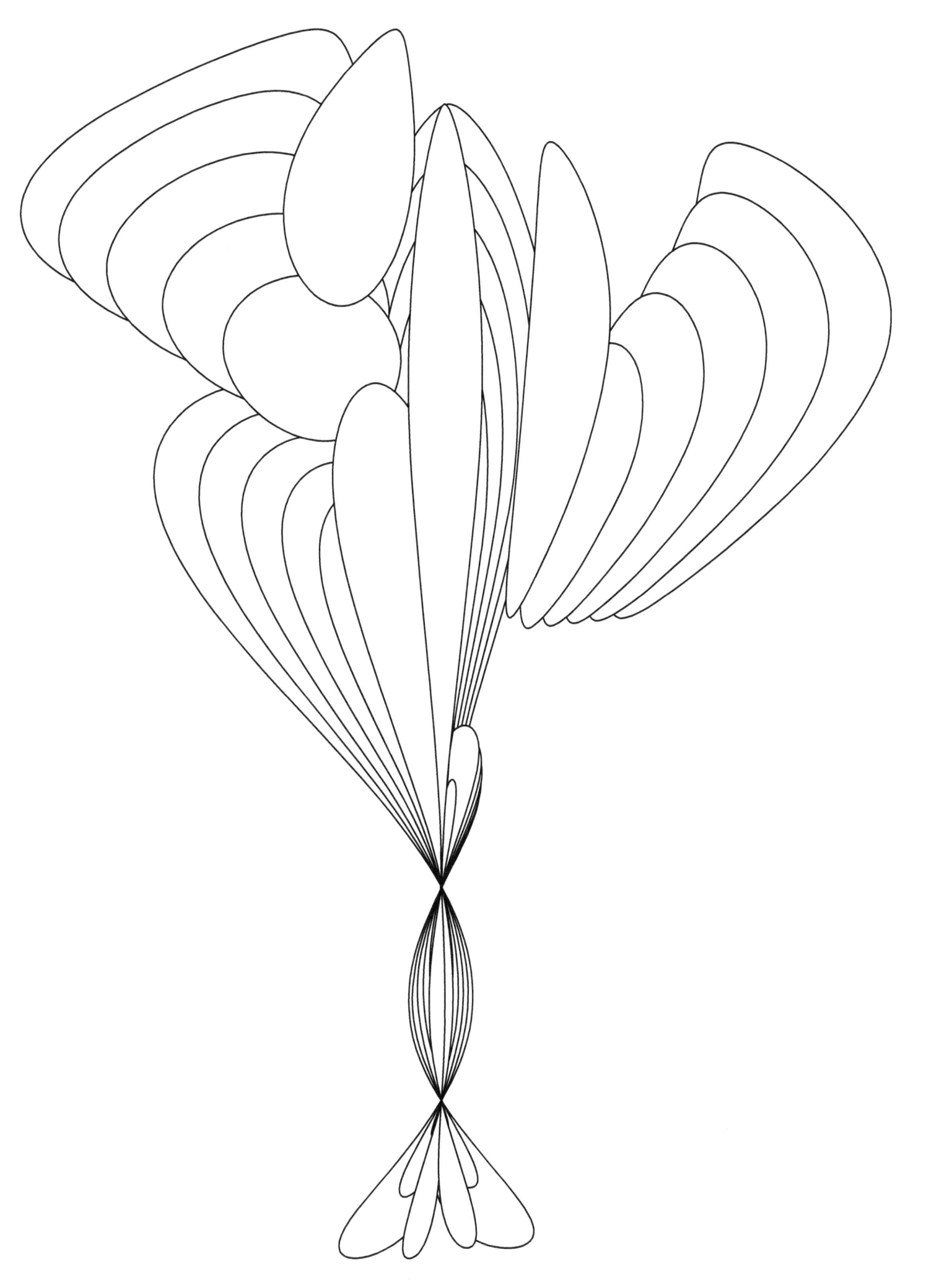

D# 1989

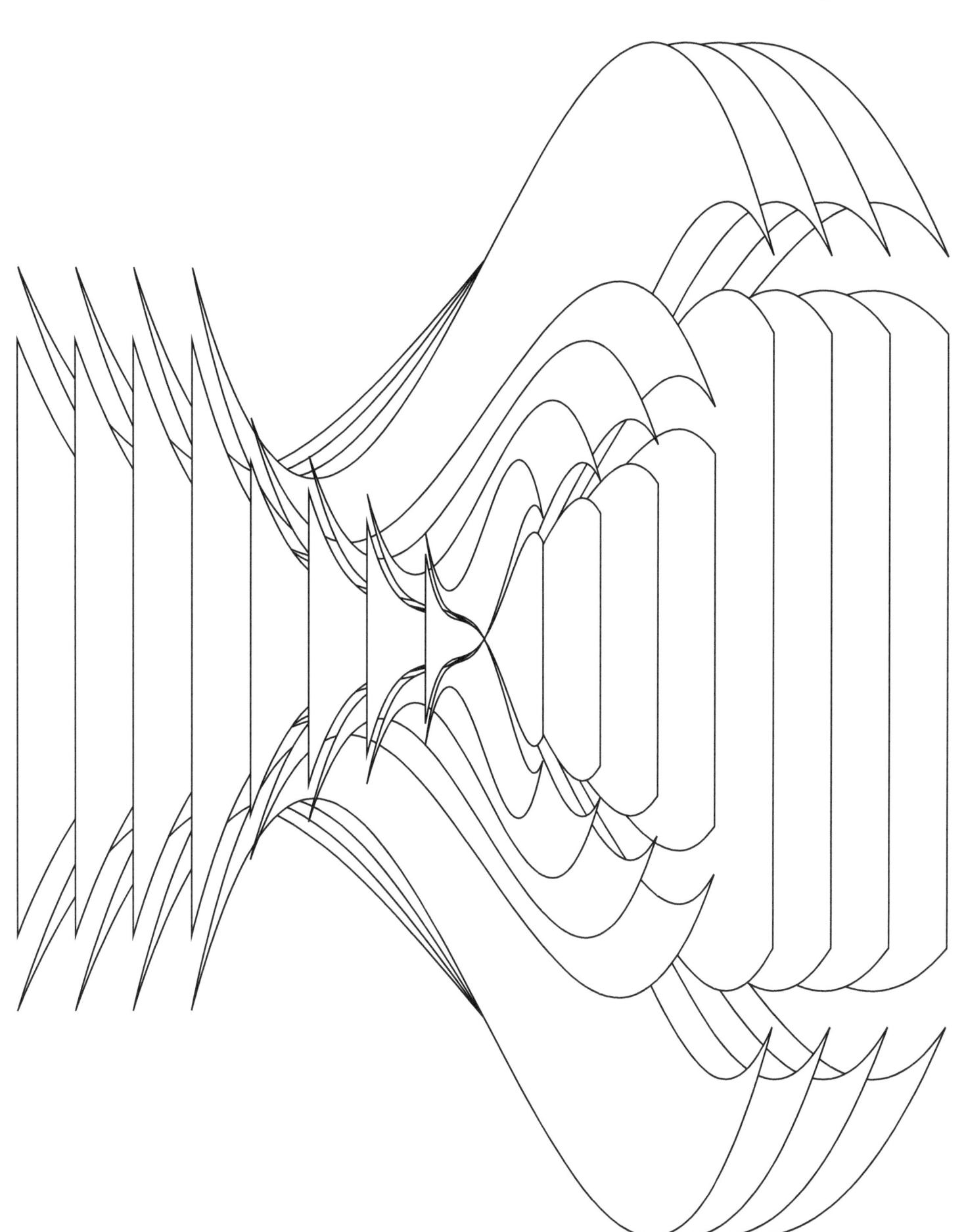

D# 2145

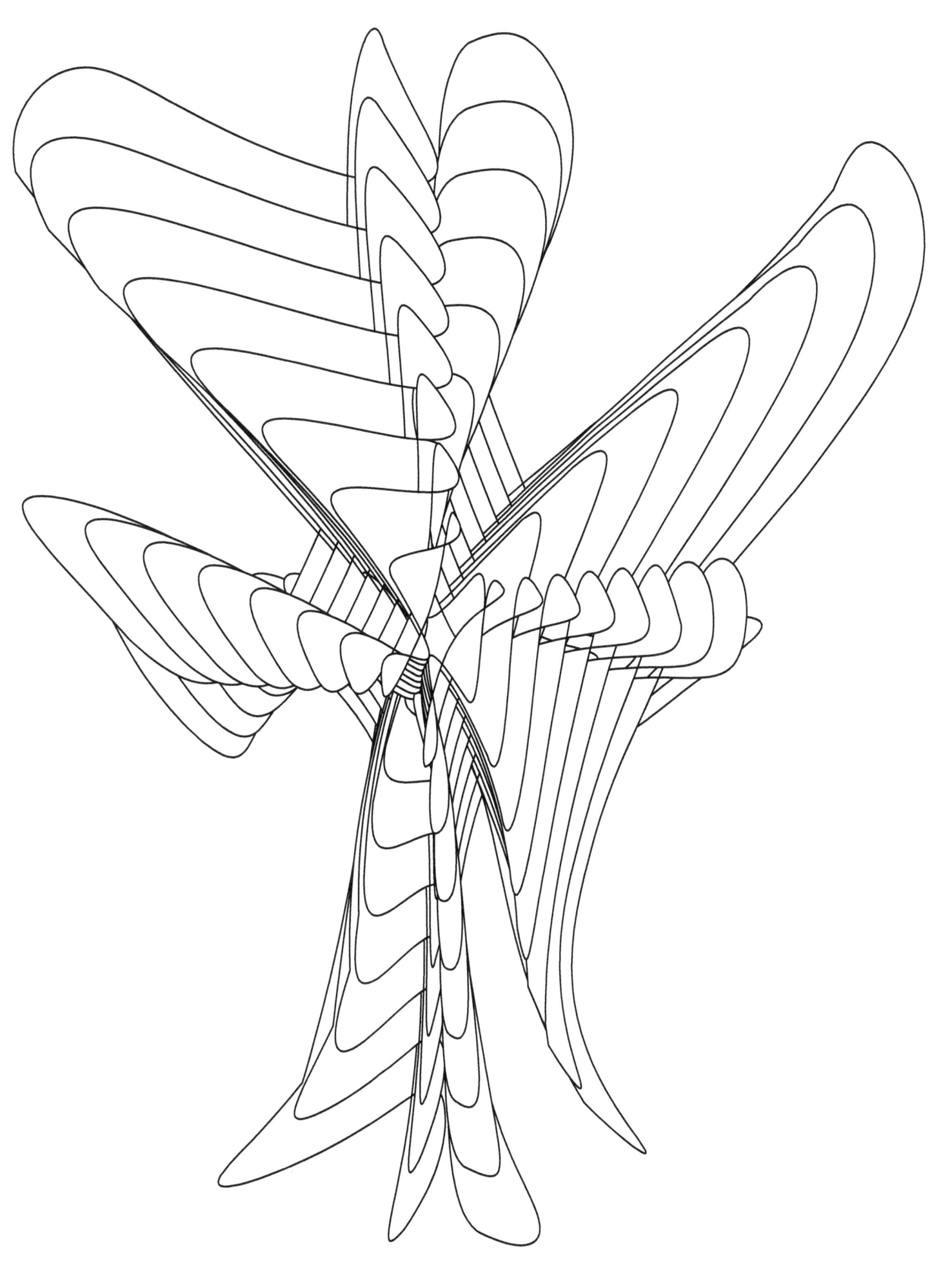

D# 1996

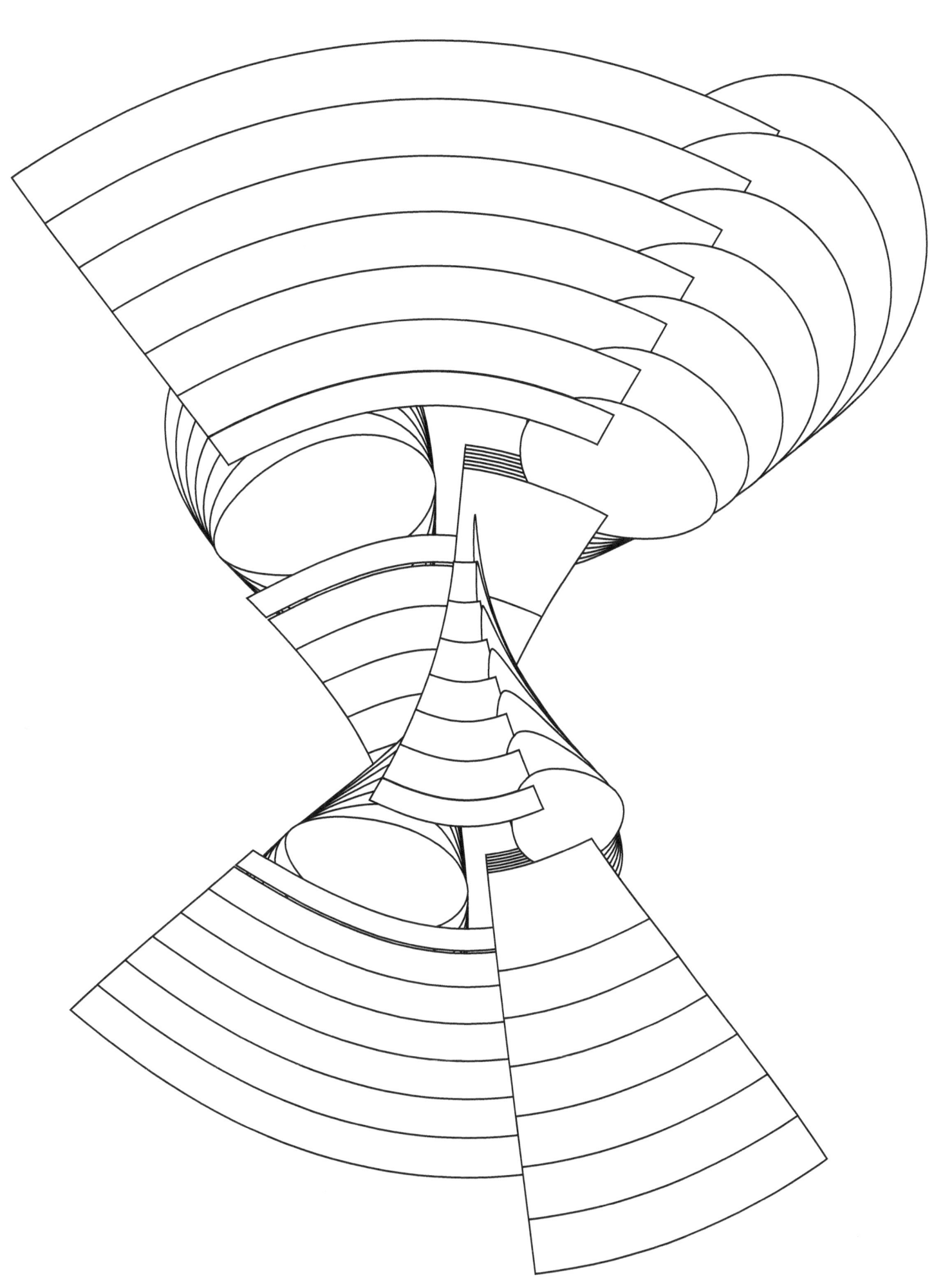

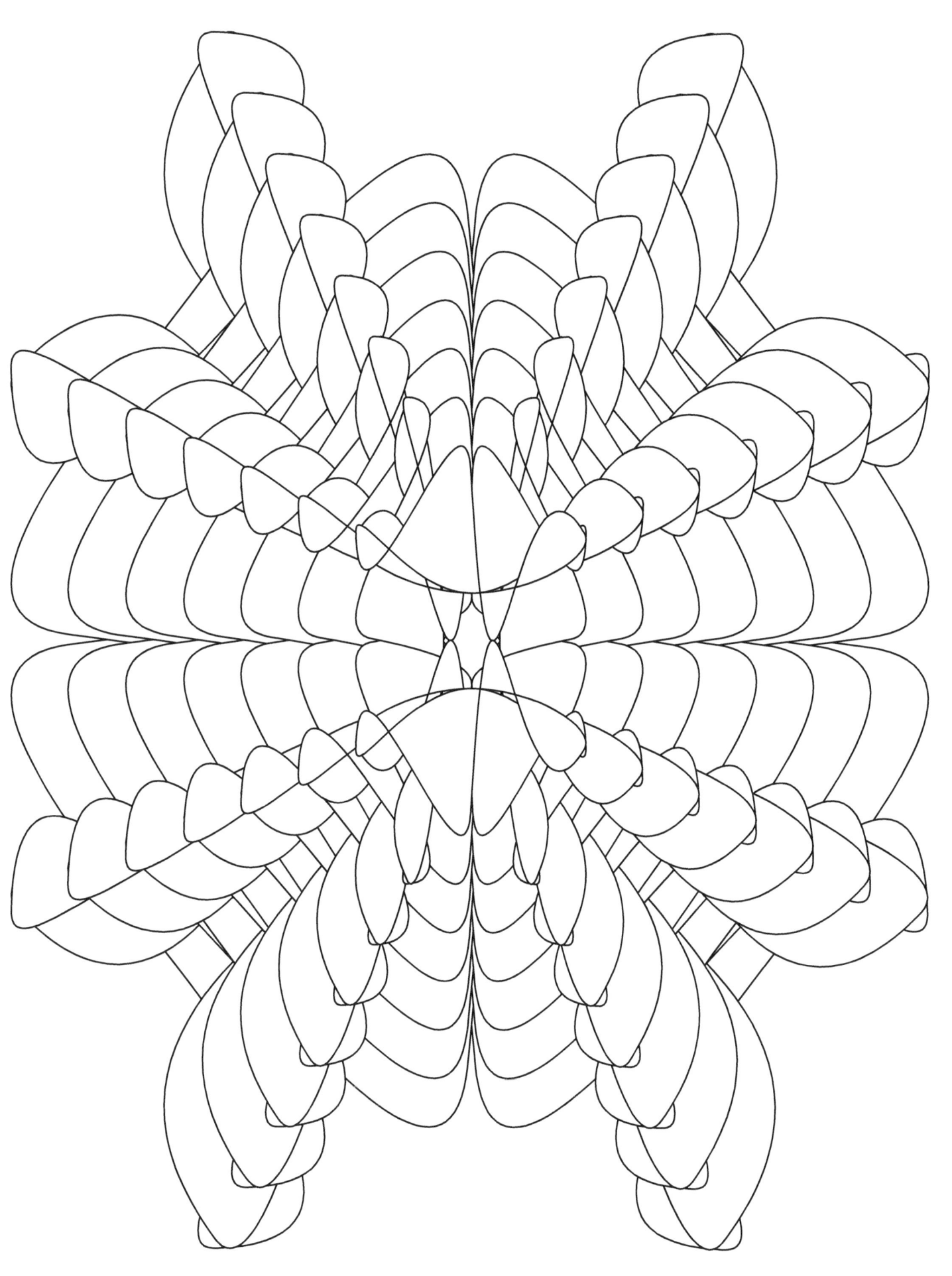

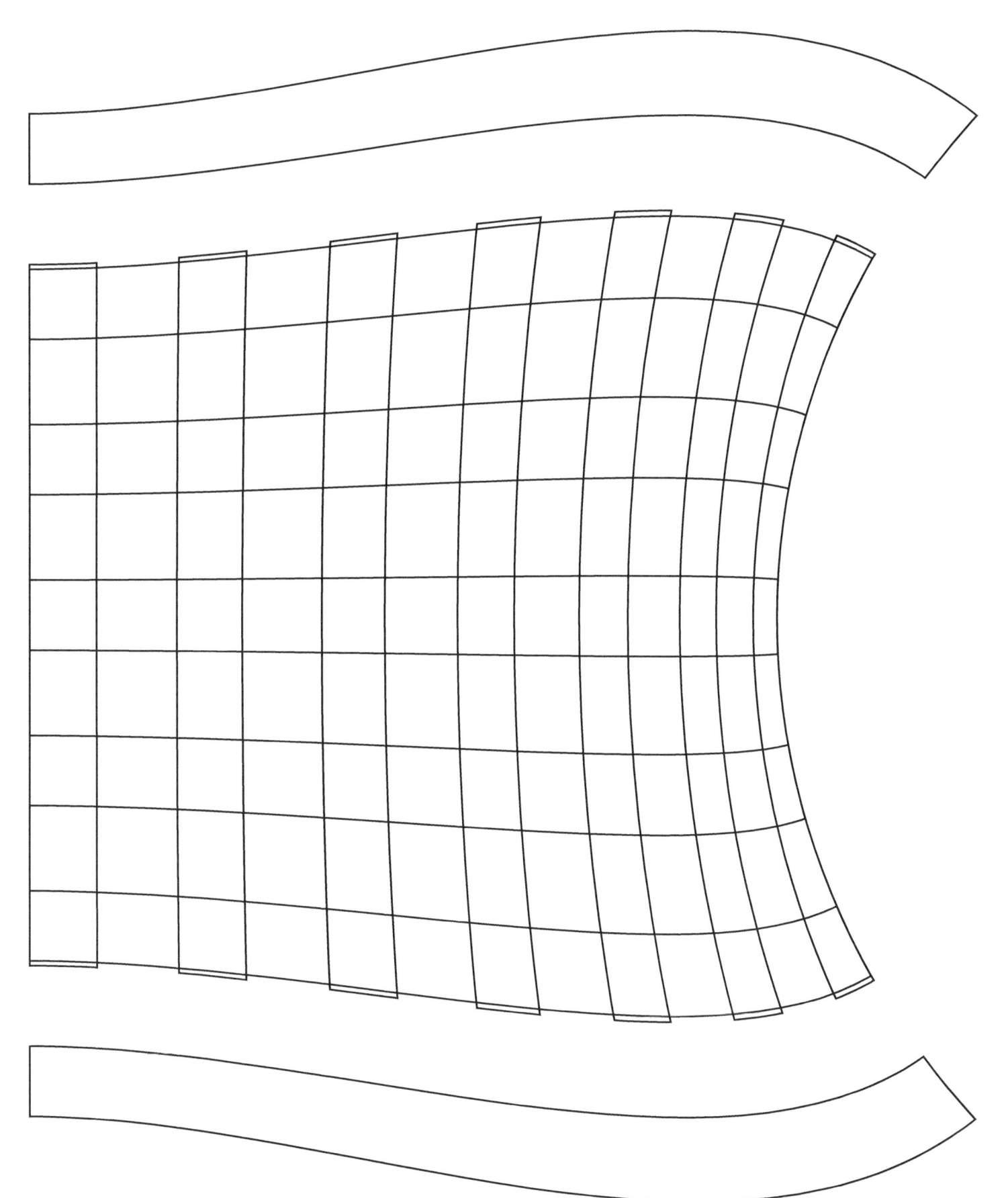

D# 72SQ

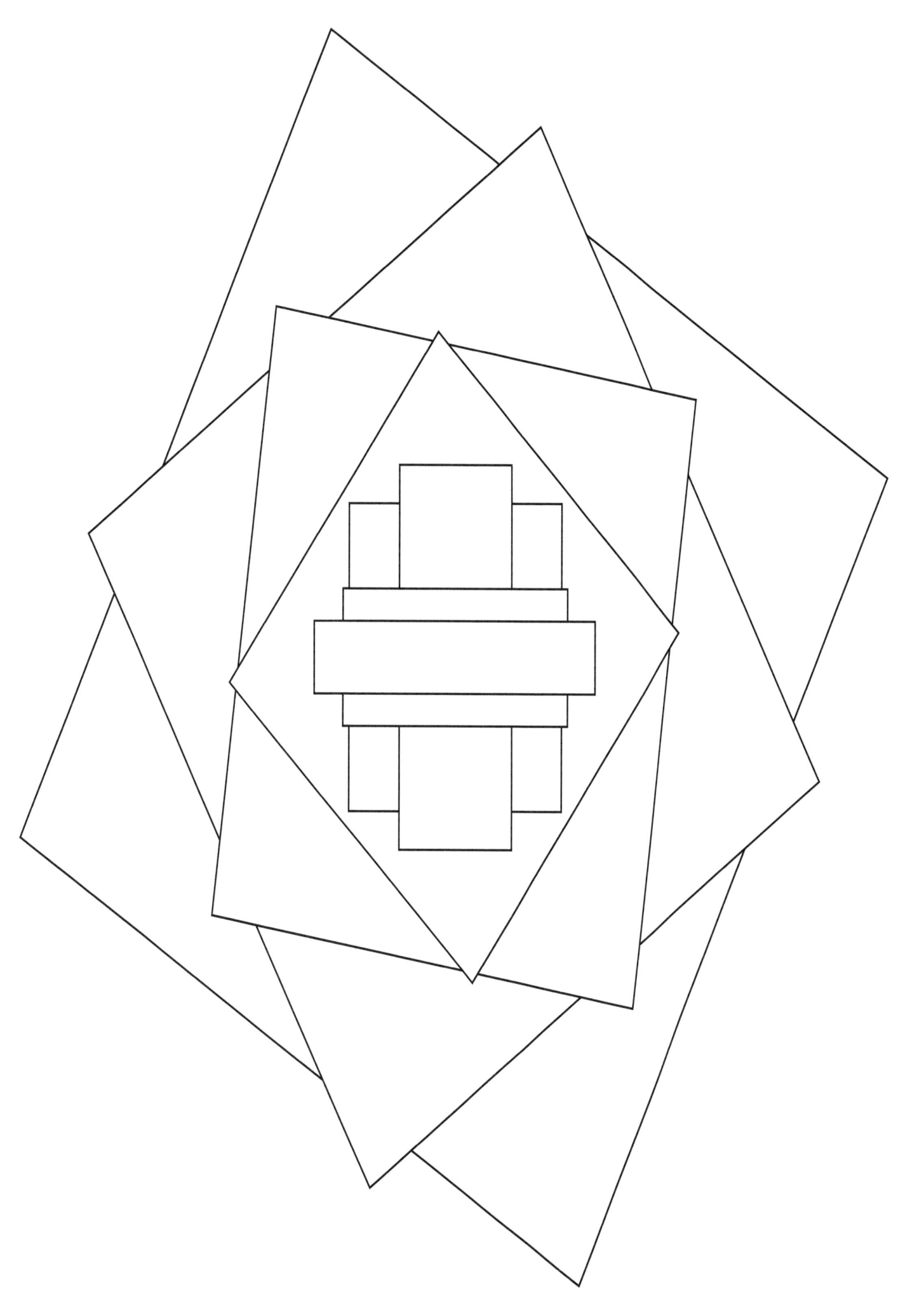

D# 91SQ

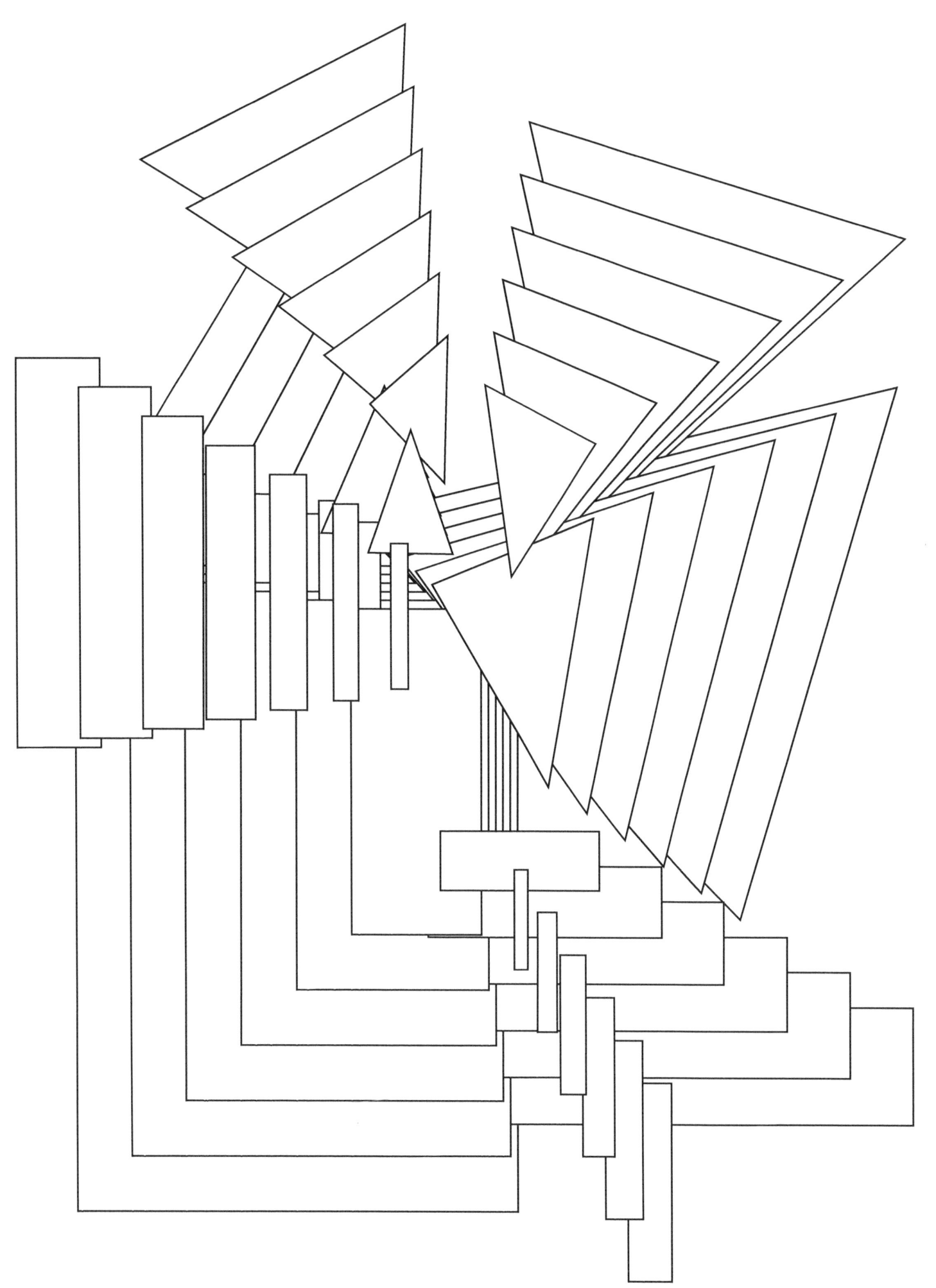

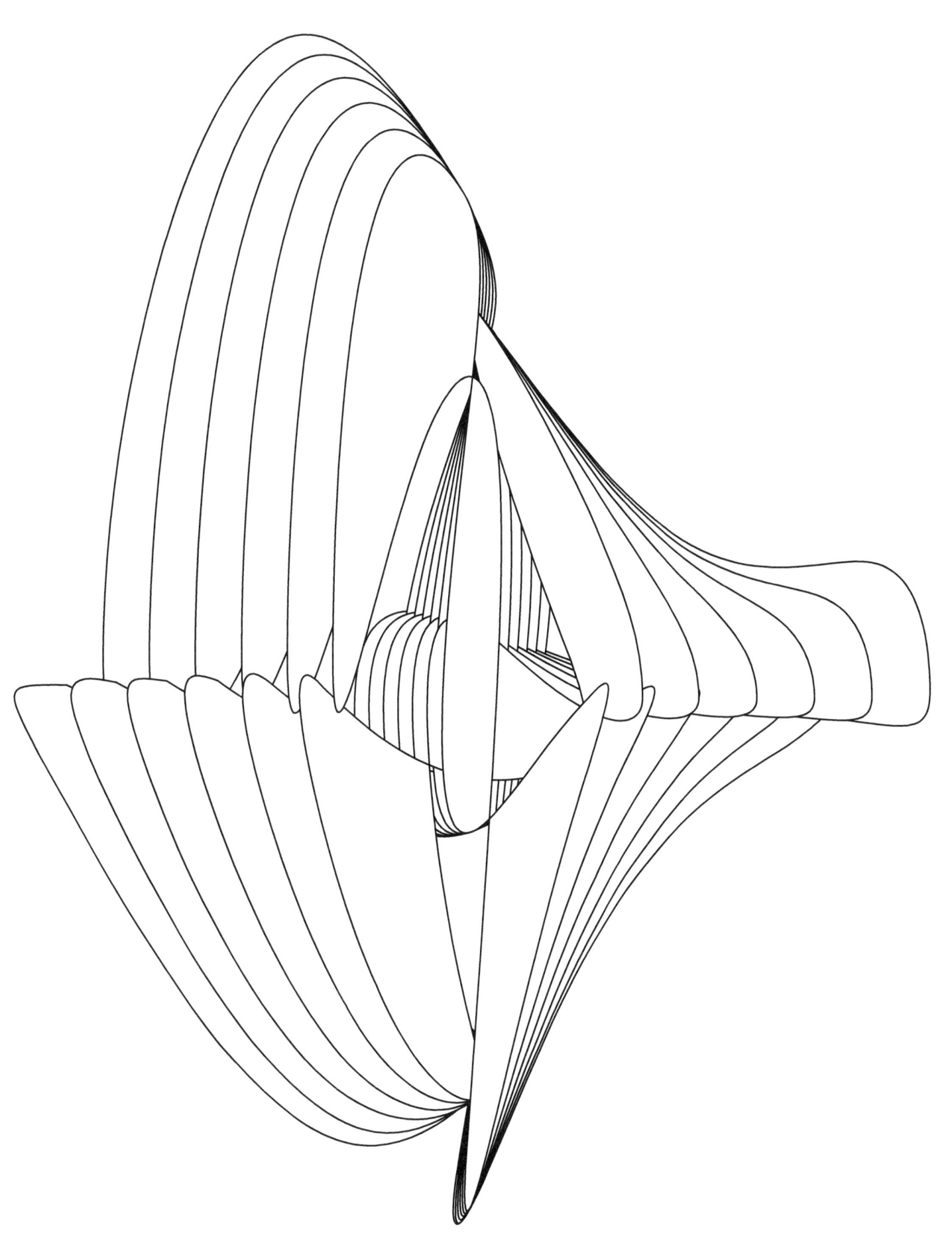

D# 1768

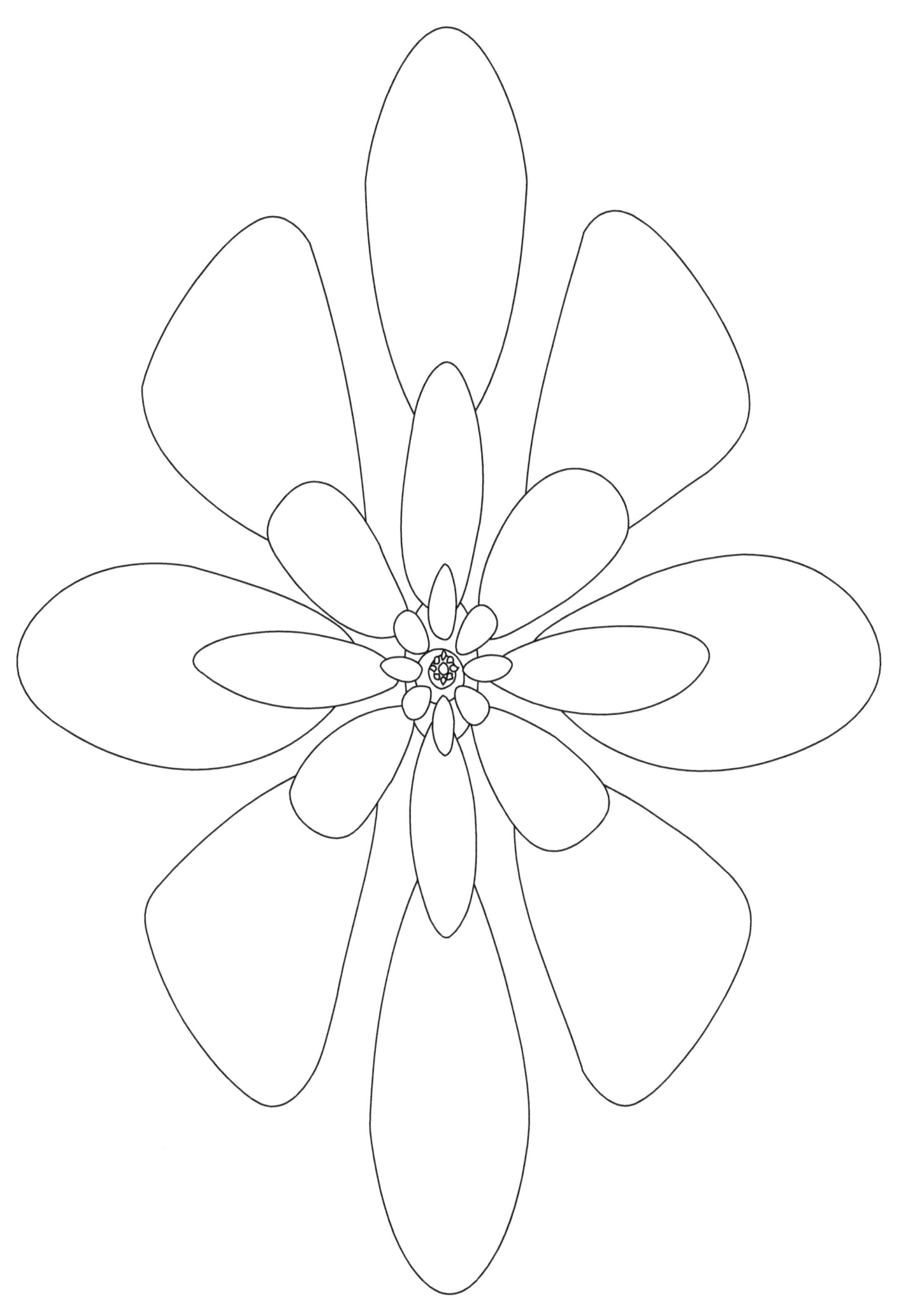

D# 2154

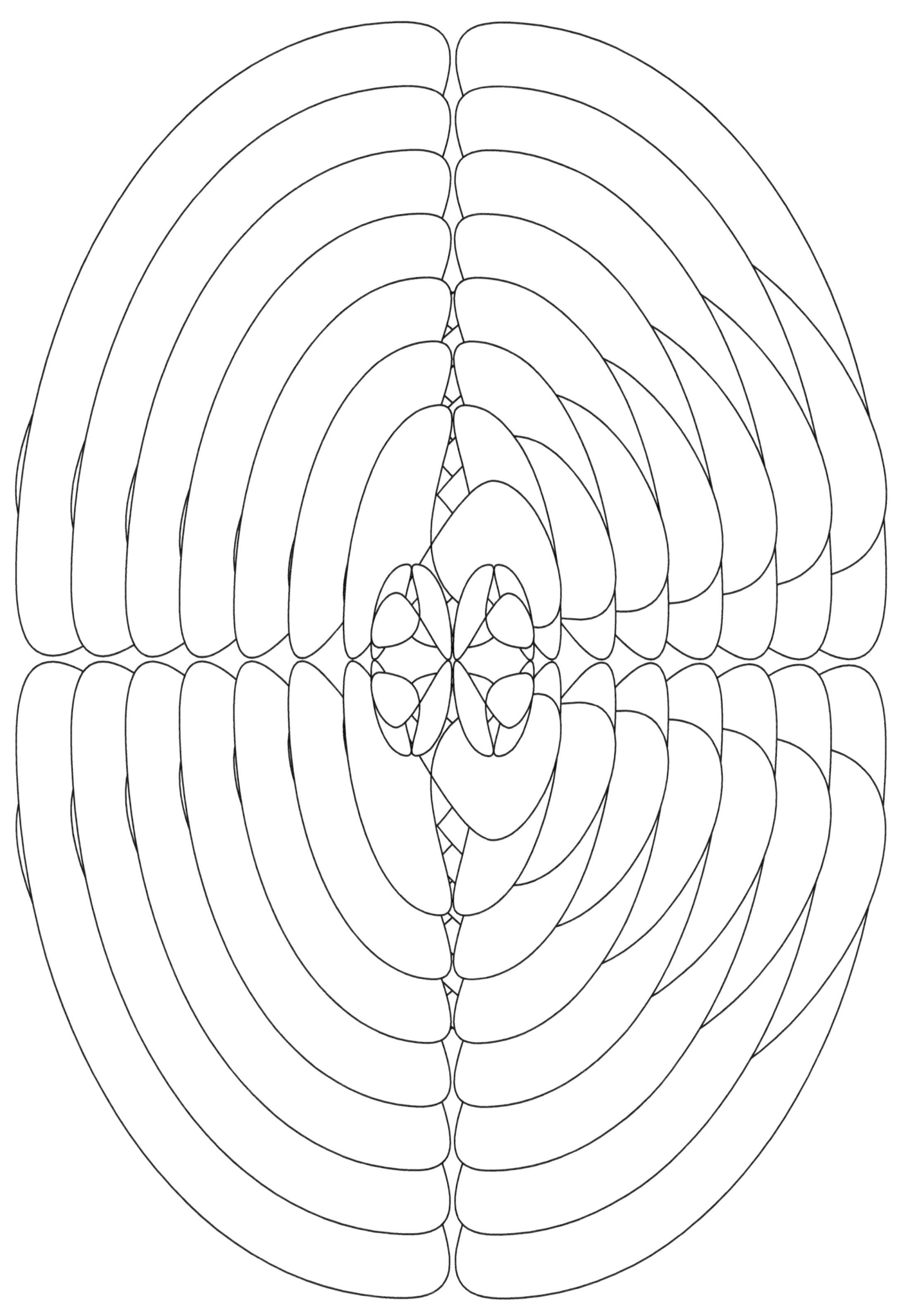

D# 2147

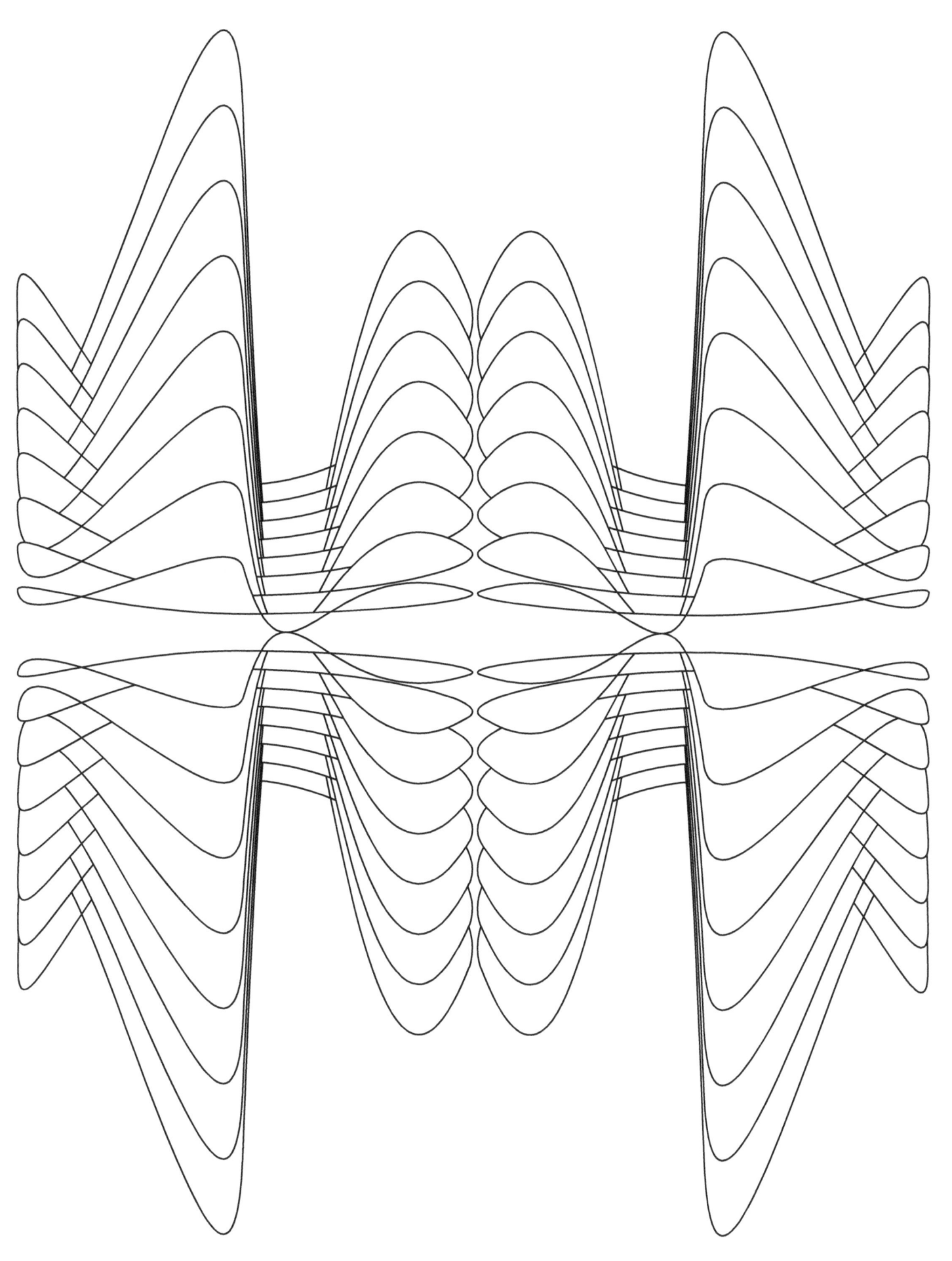

D# 2051

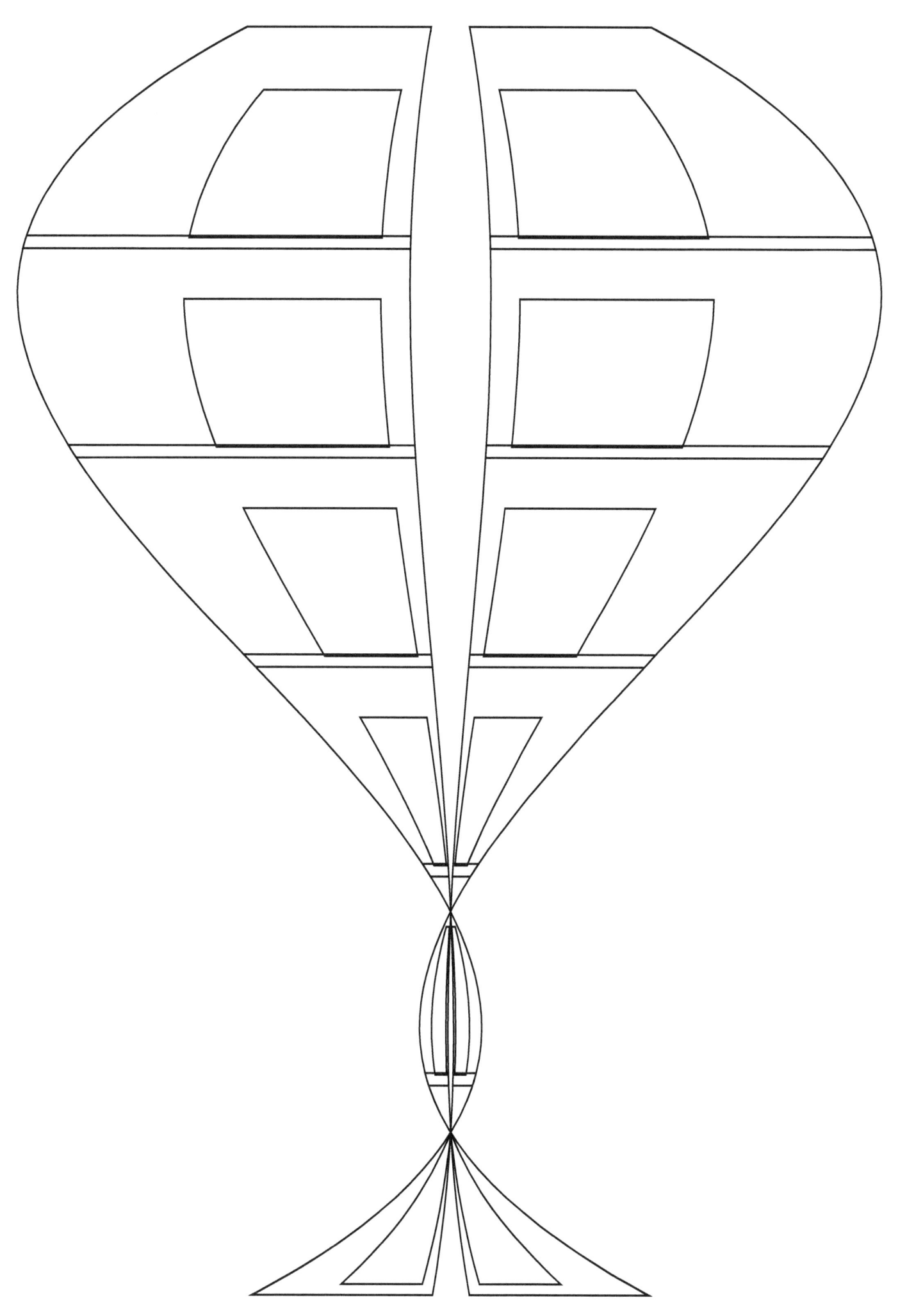

D# 1964

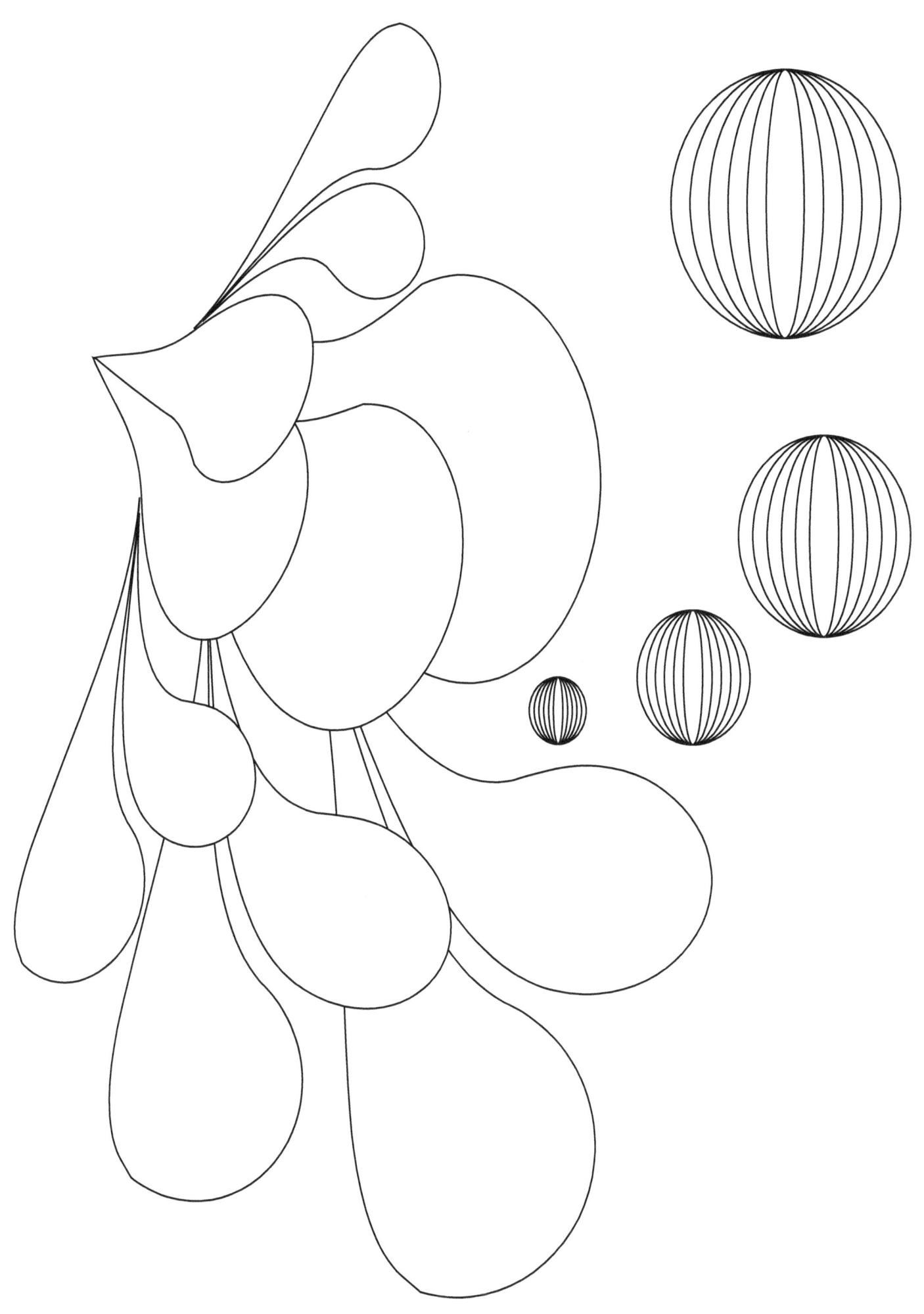

D# 1972

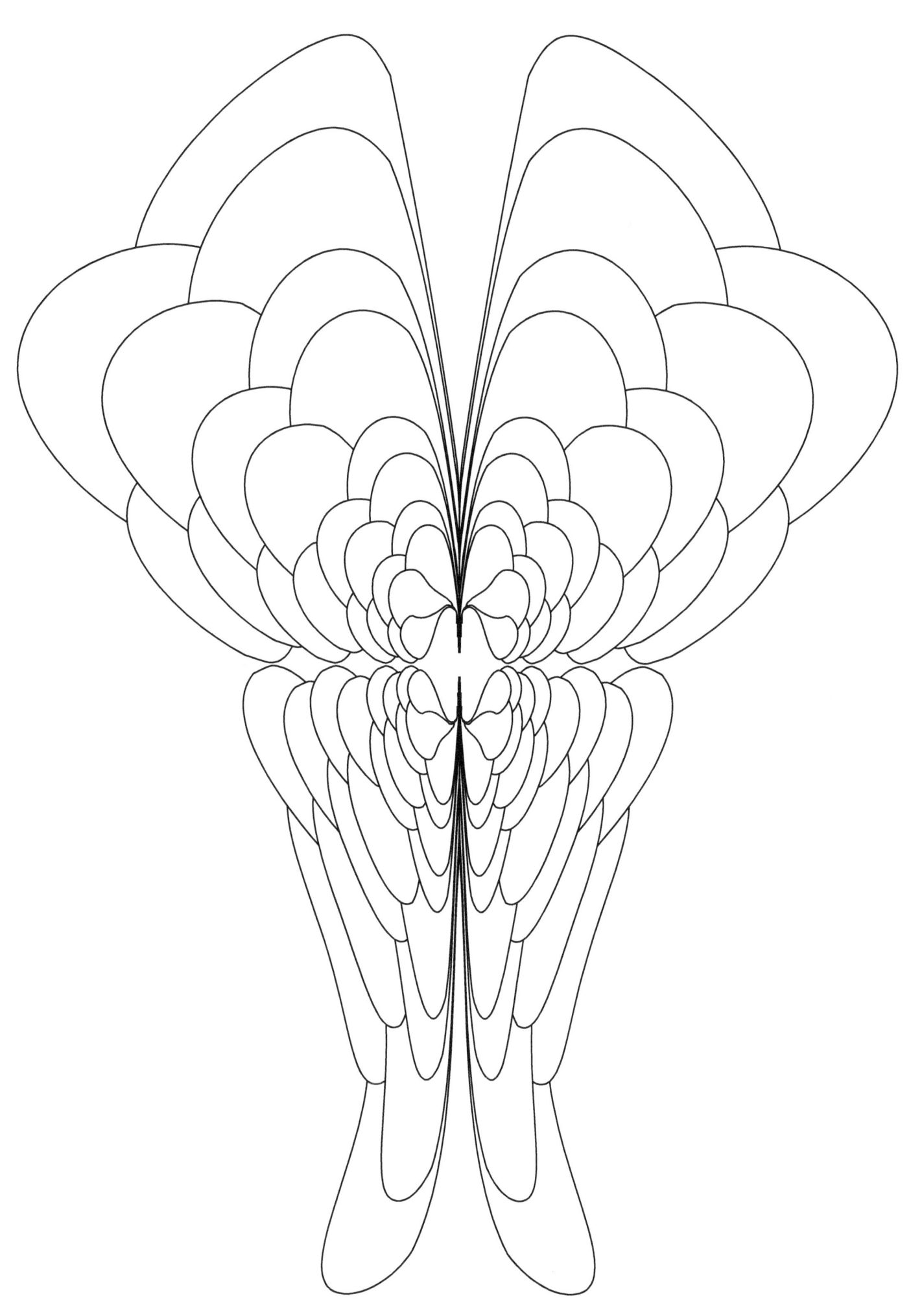

D# 2146

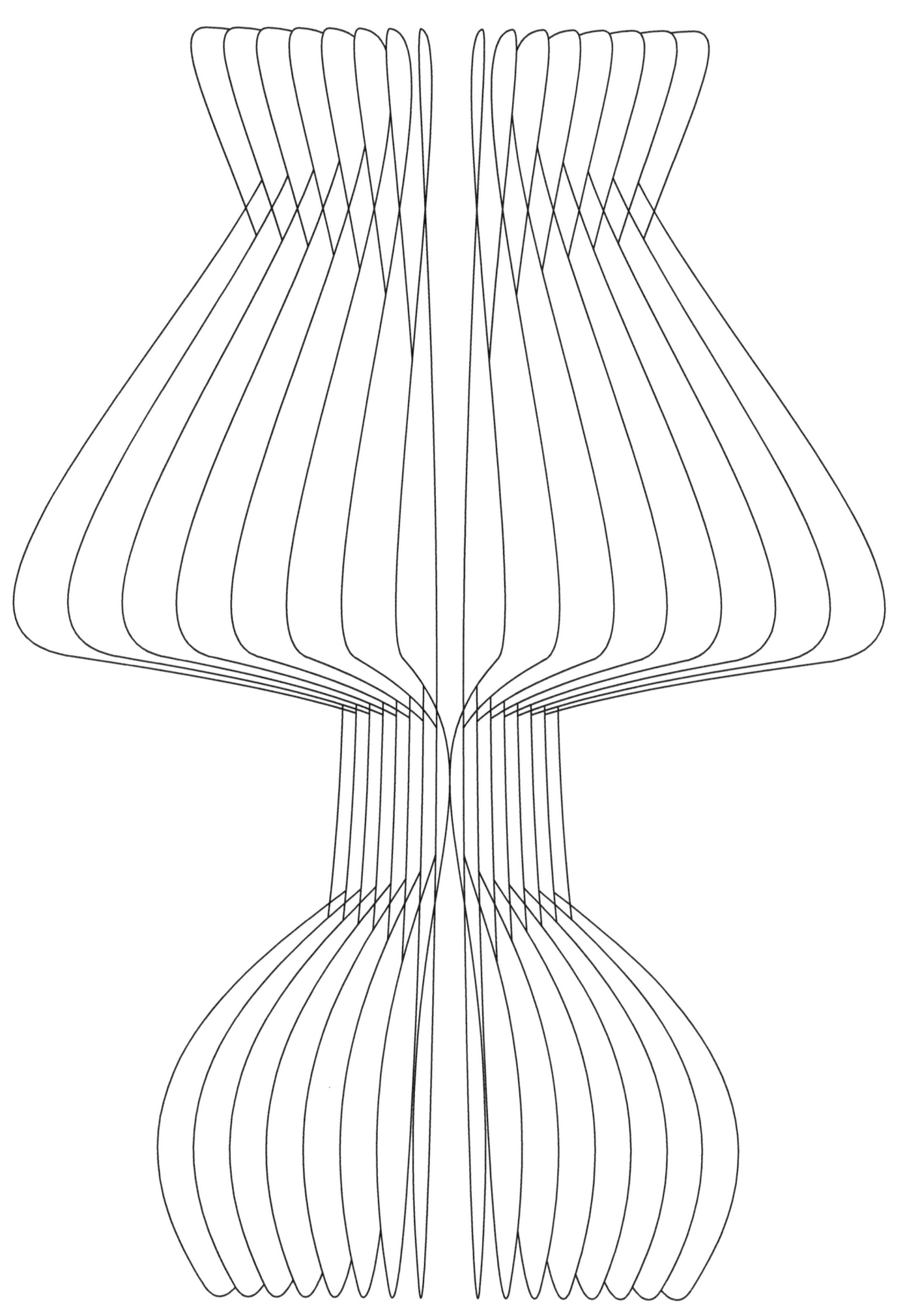

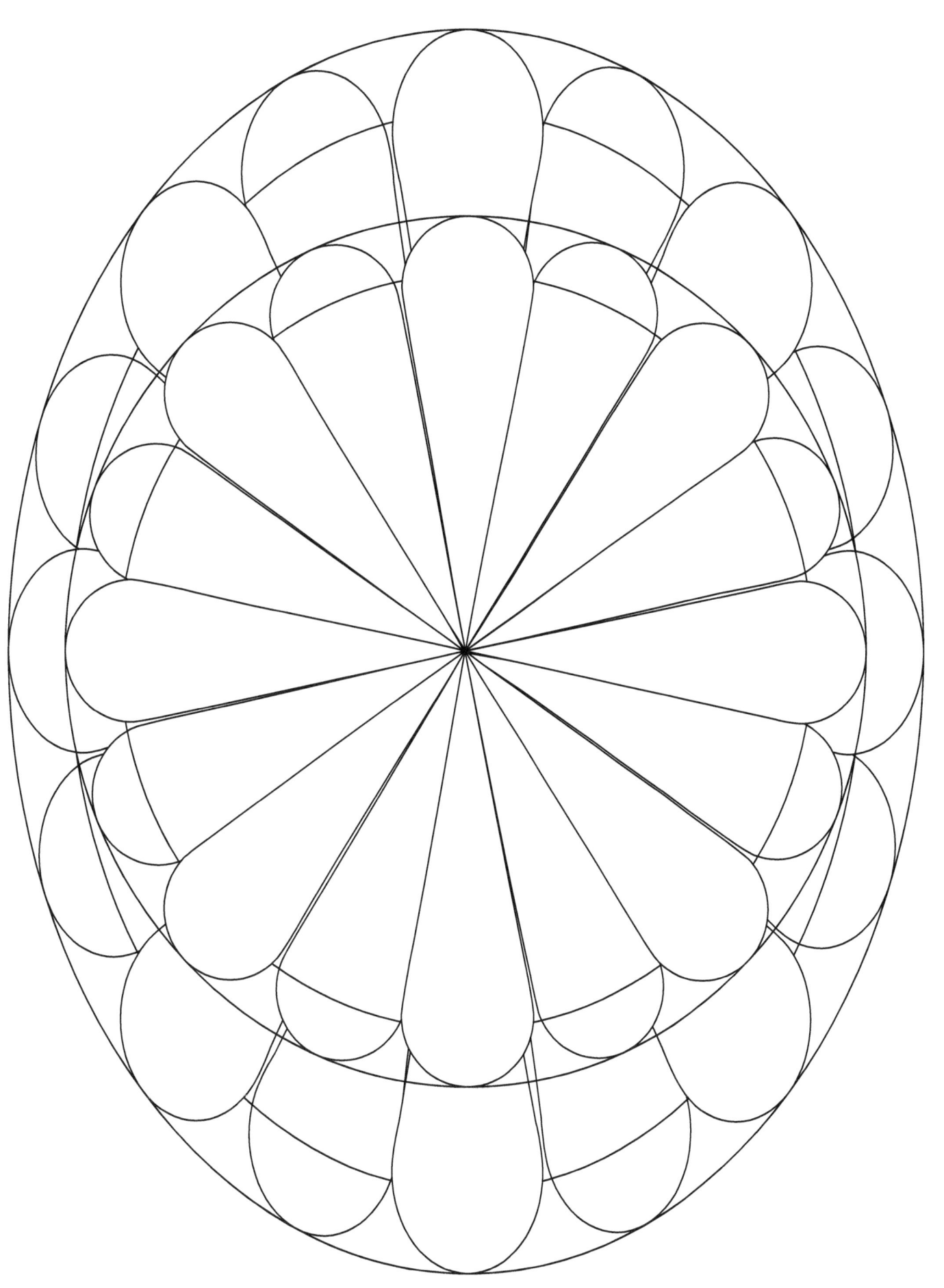

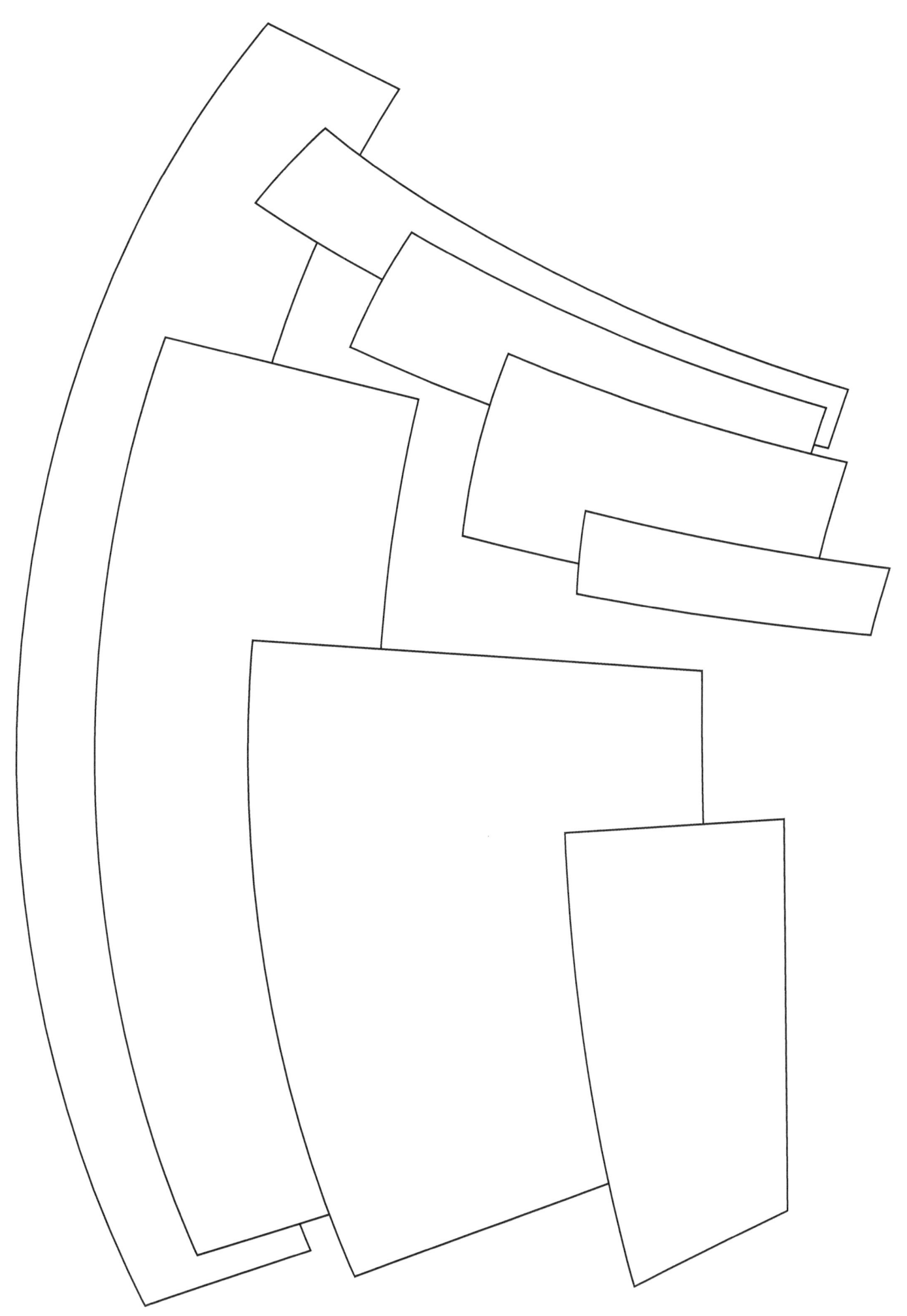

D# 2139

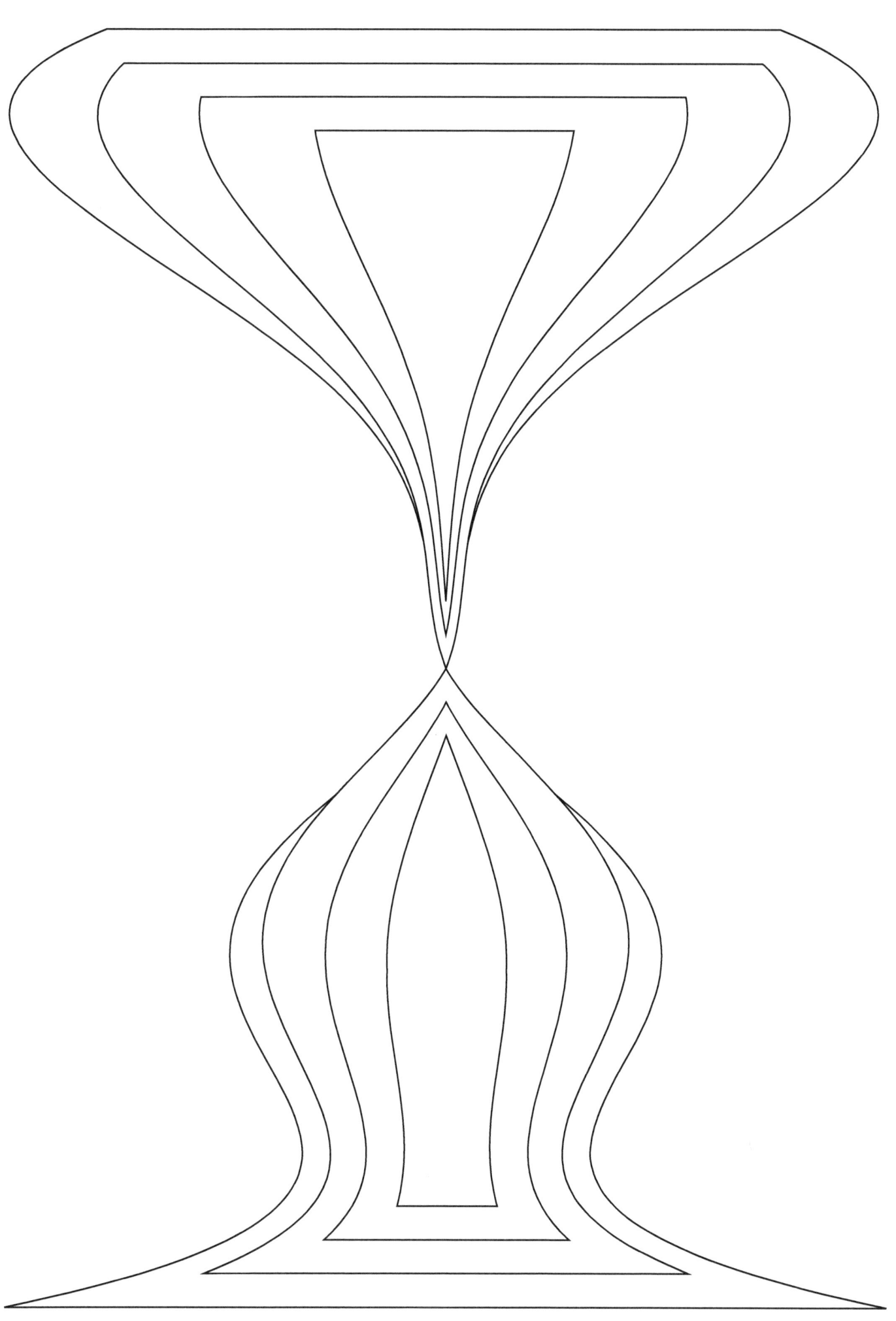

D# 1947

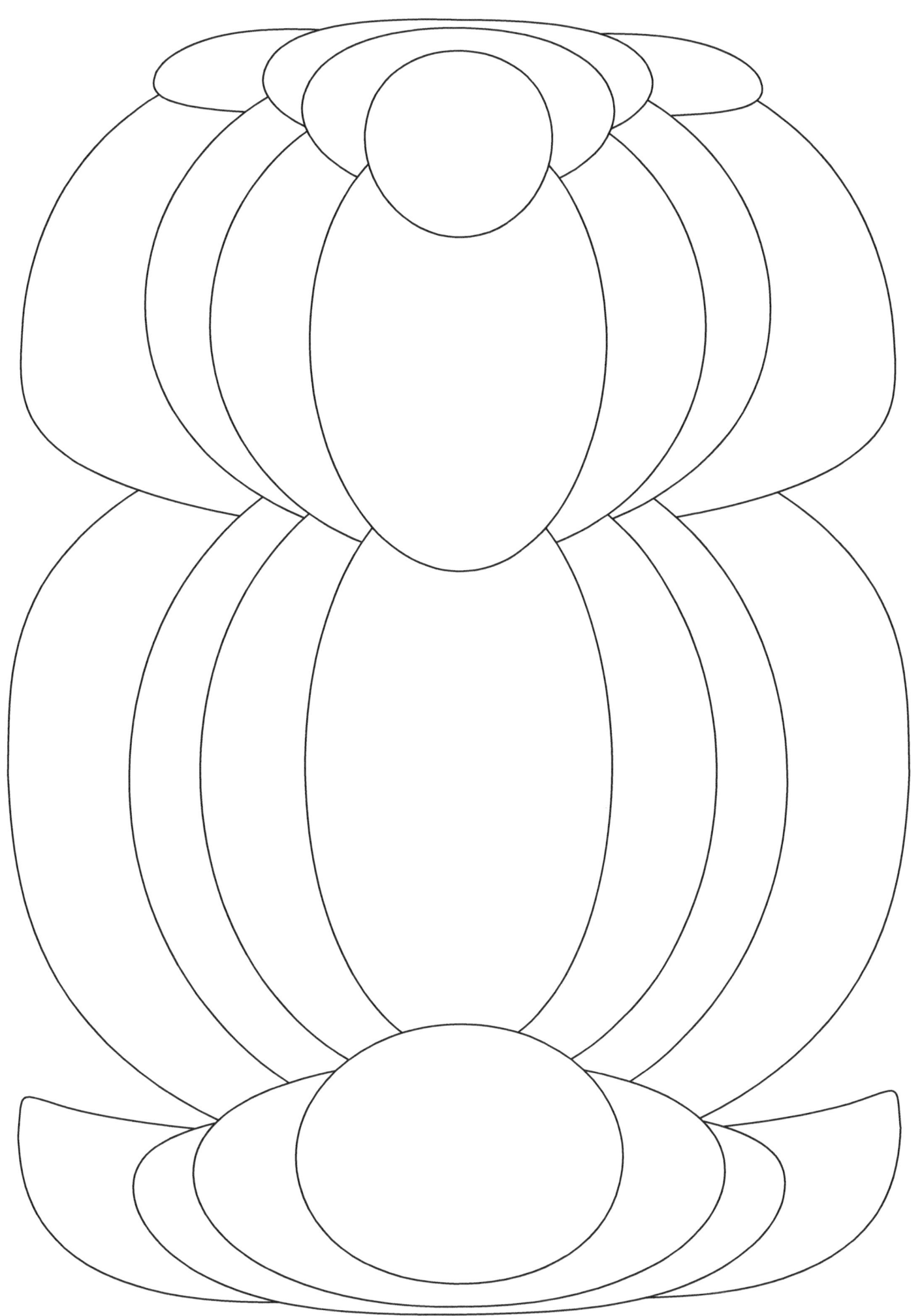

D# 1960

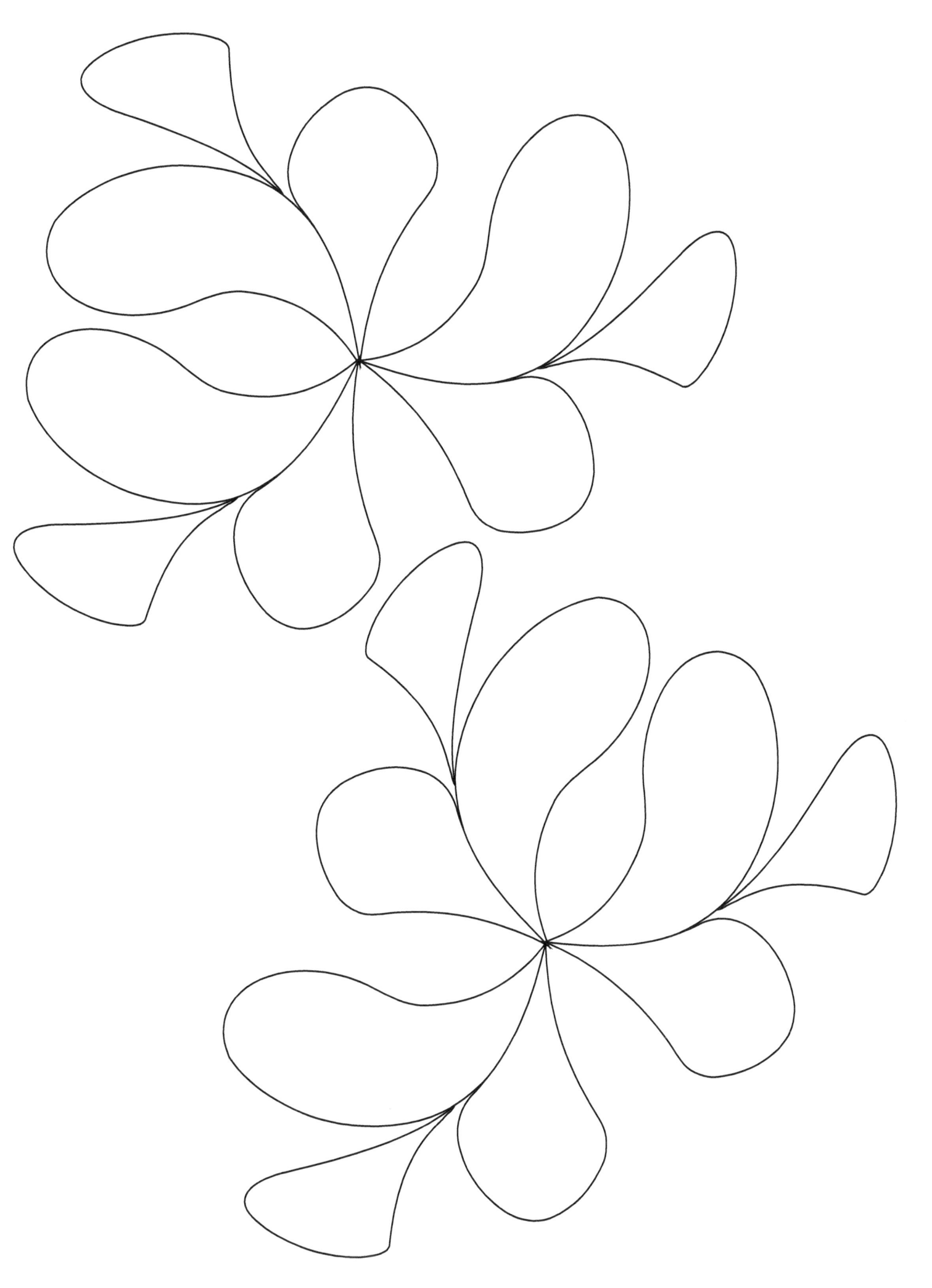

D# 2131

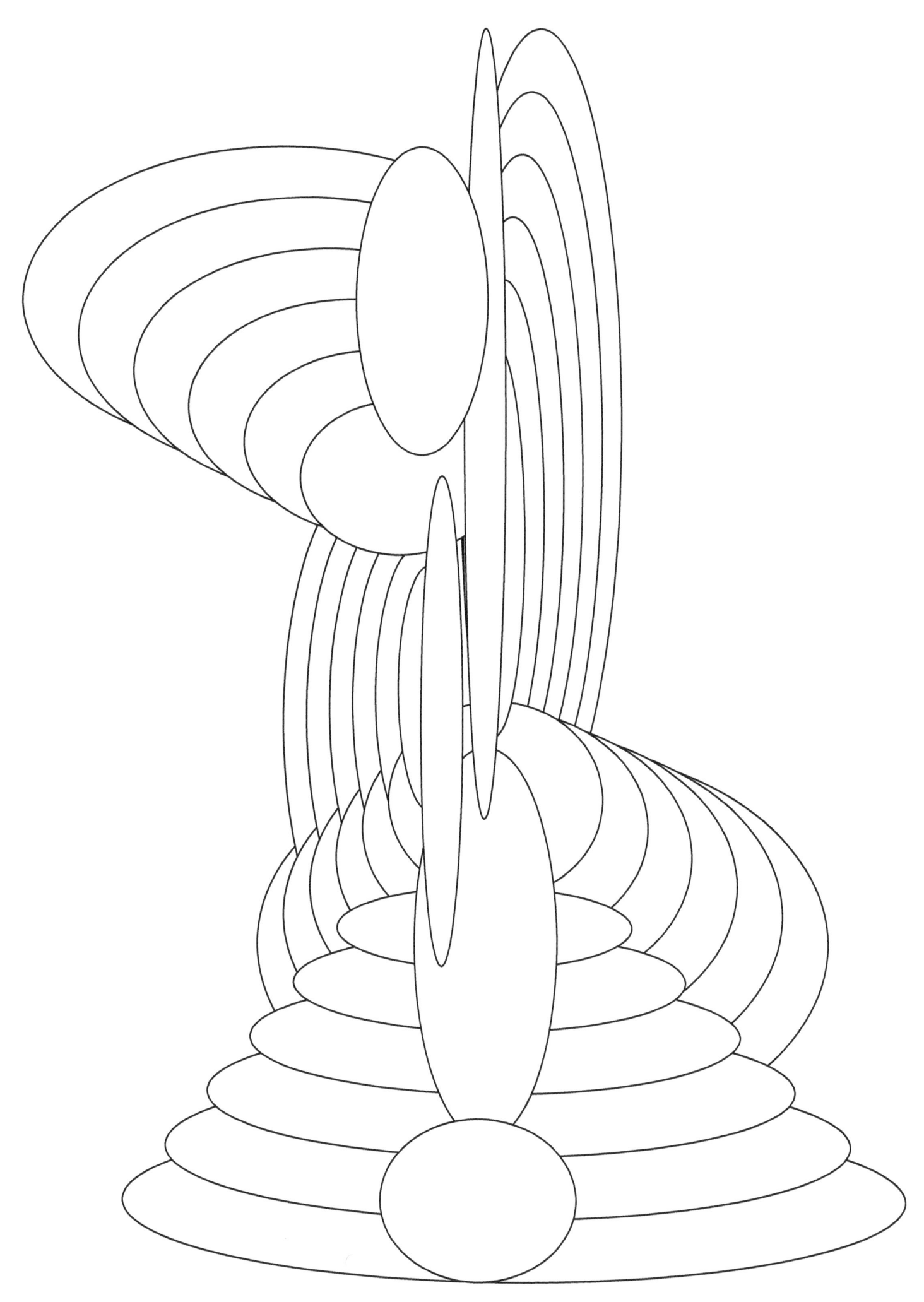

D# 1975

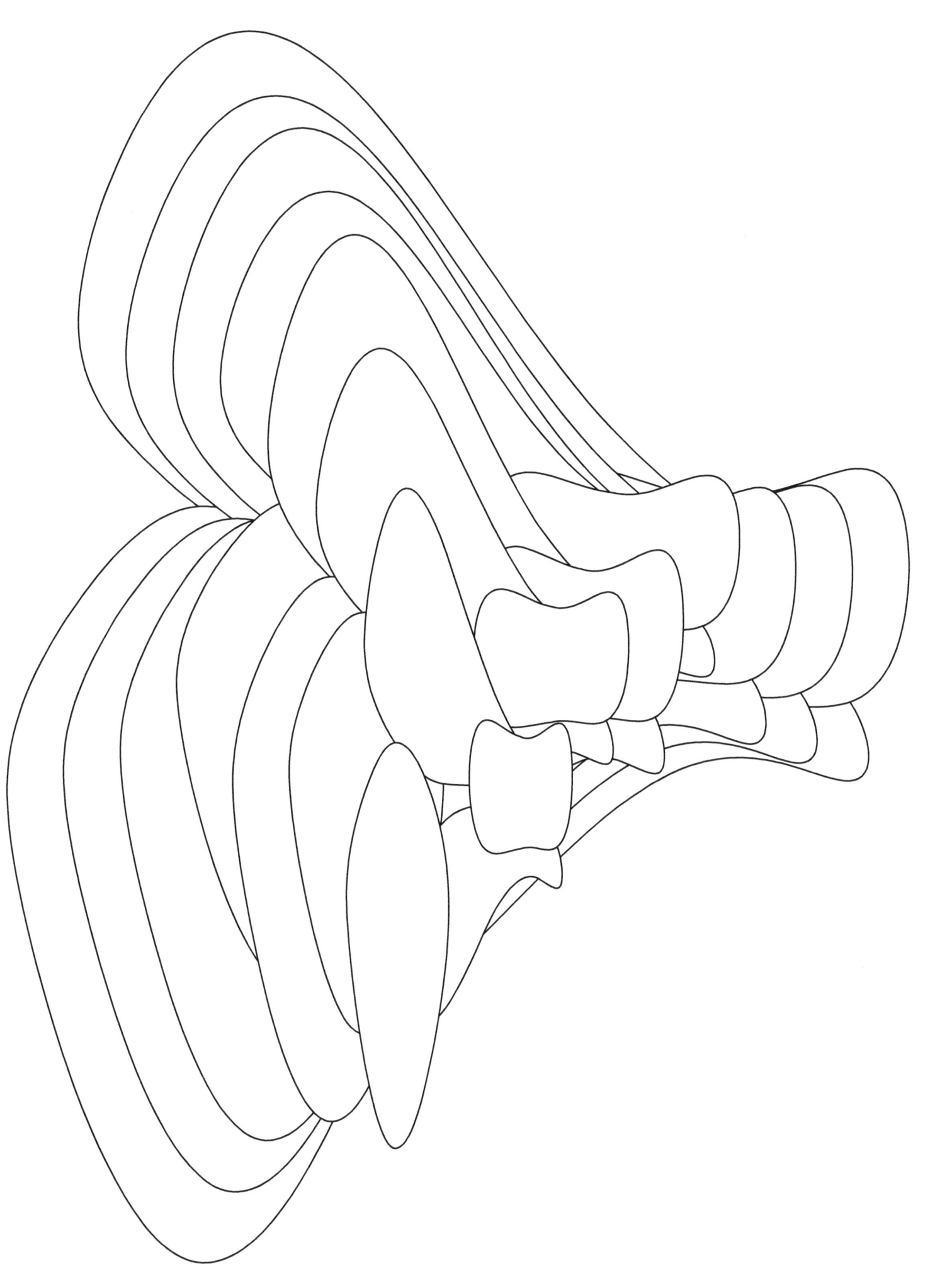

D# 1965

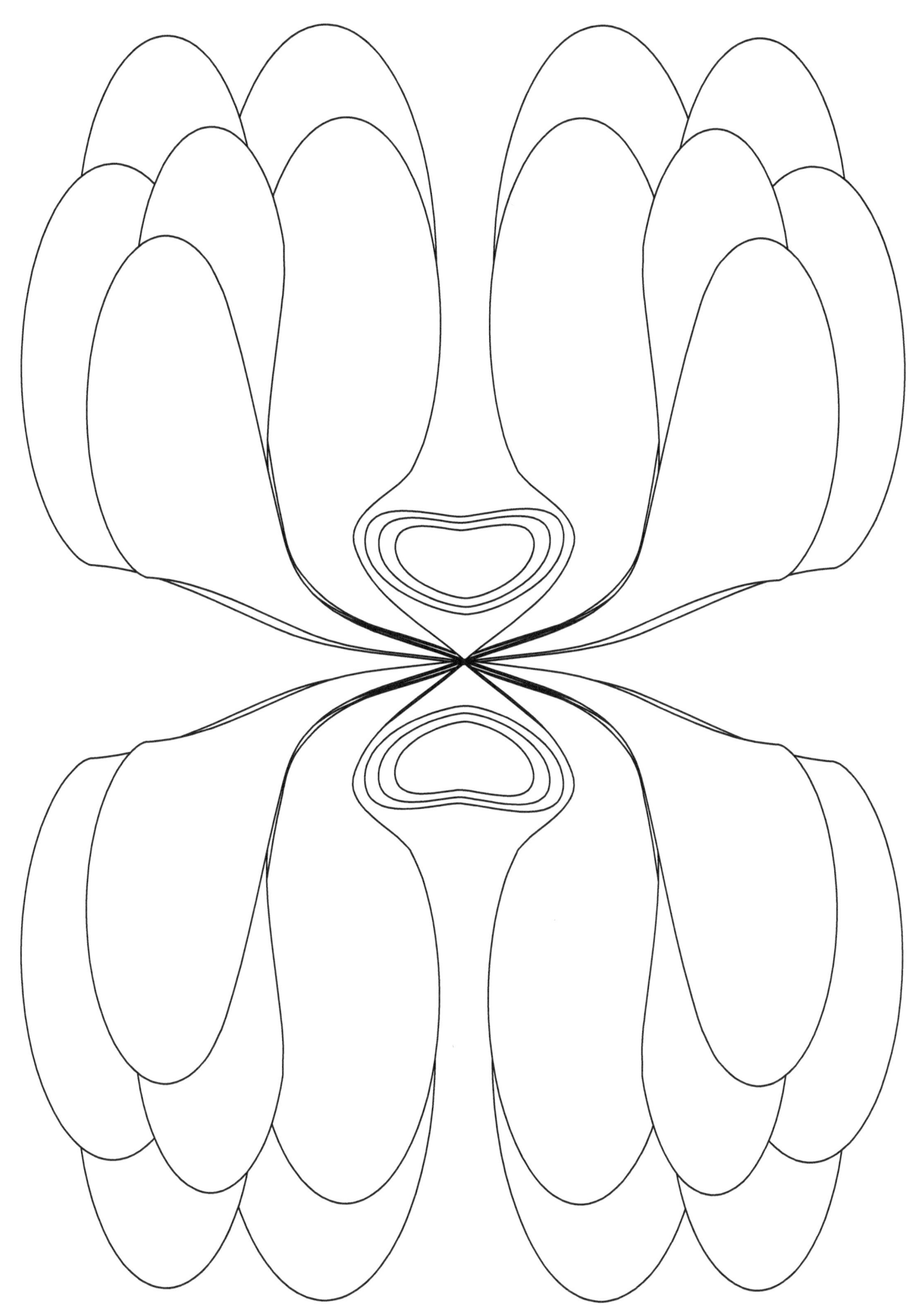

D# 2057

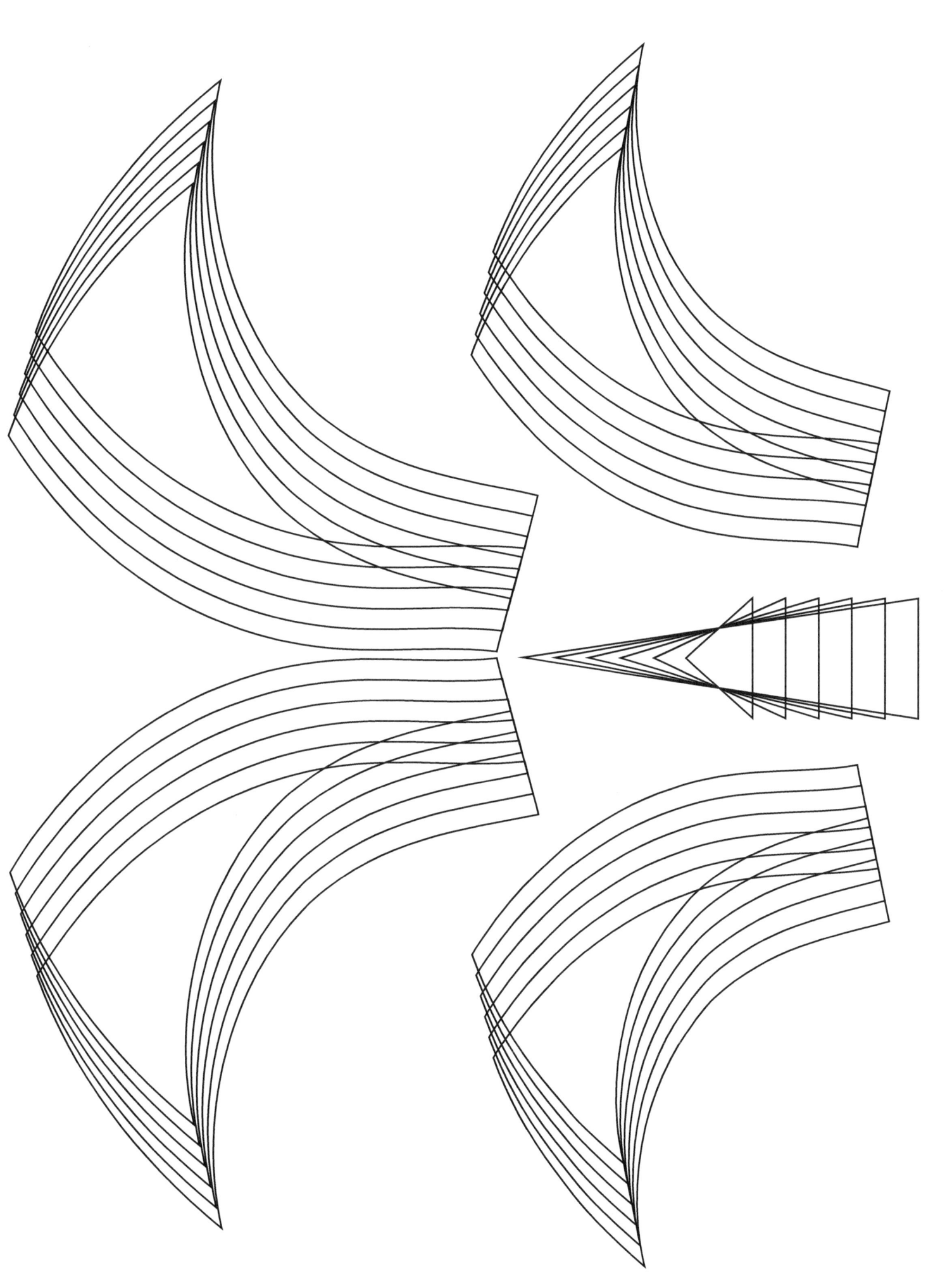

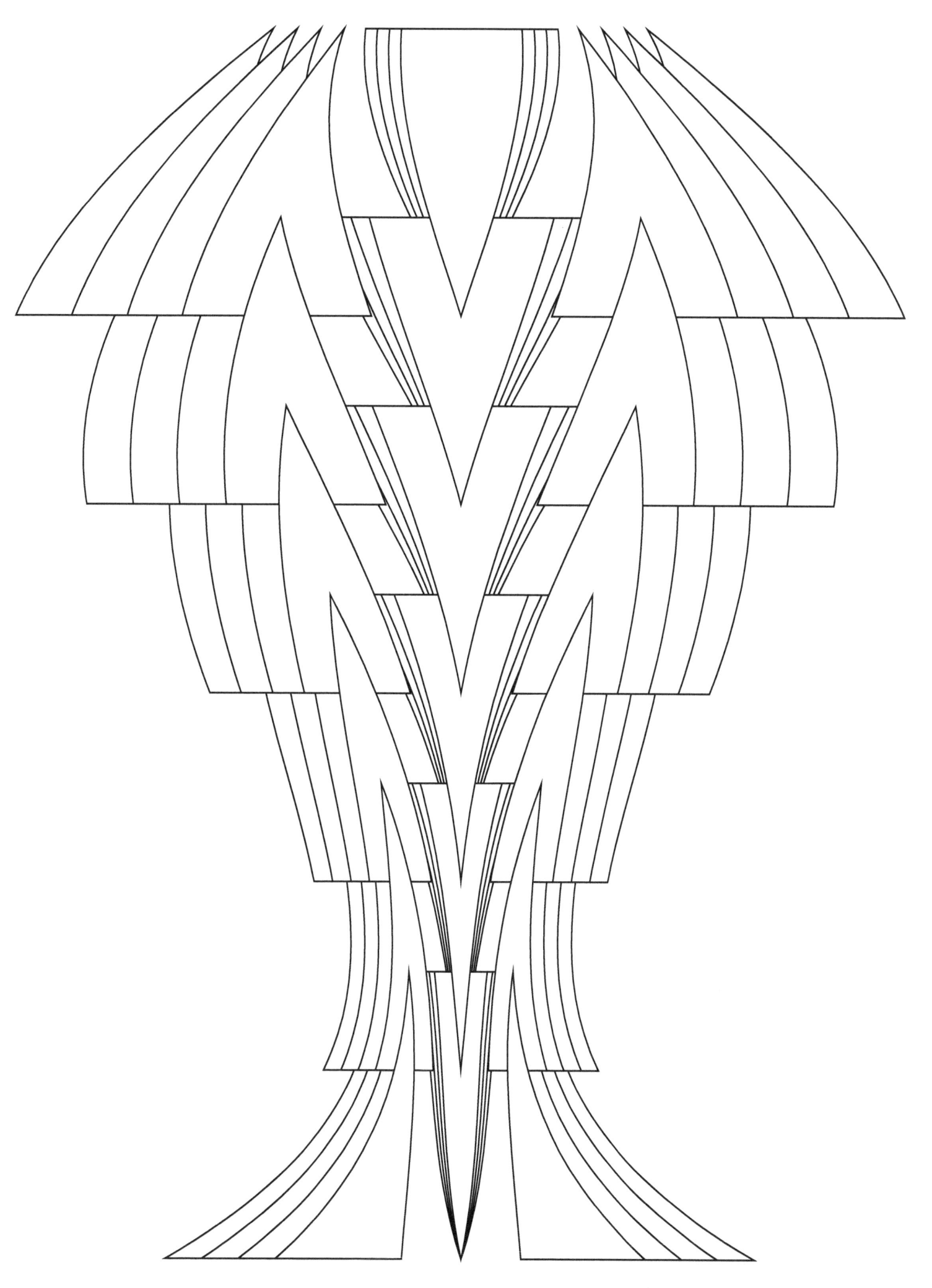

D# 97SQ

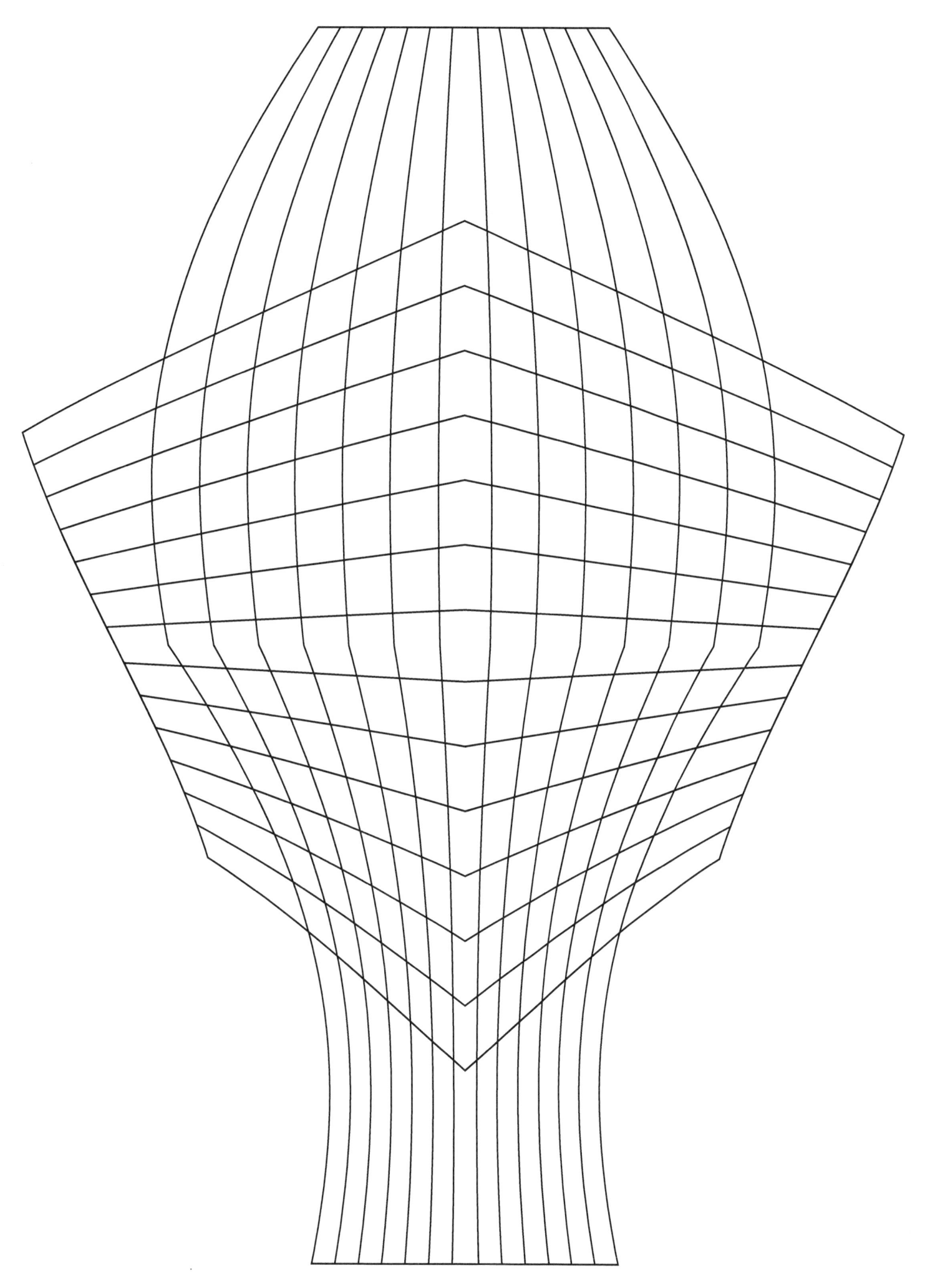

D# 1684

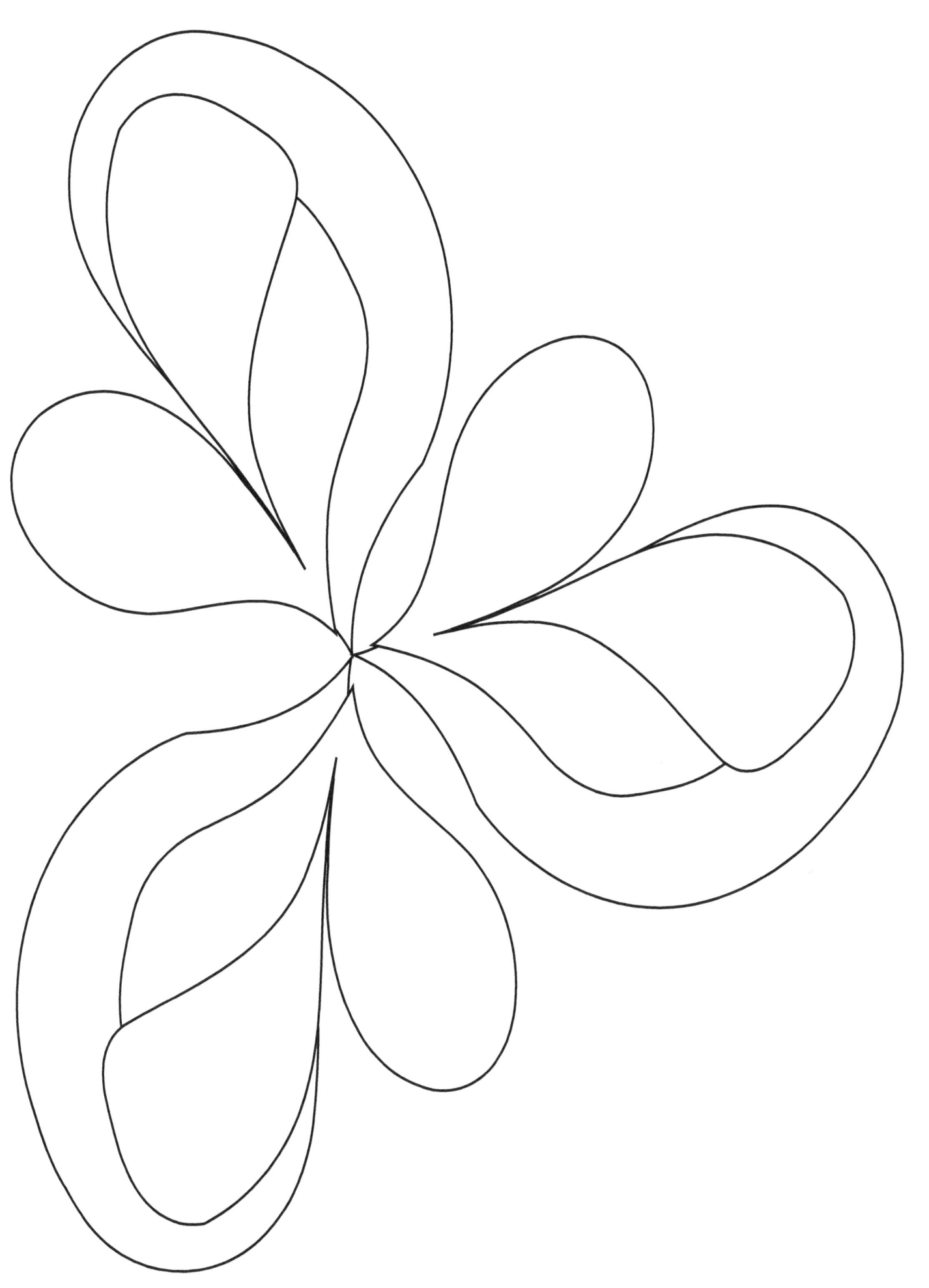

D# 2062

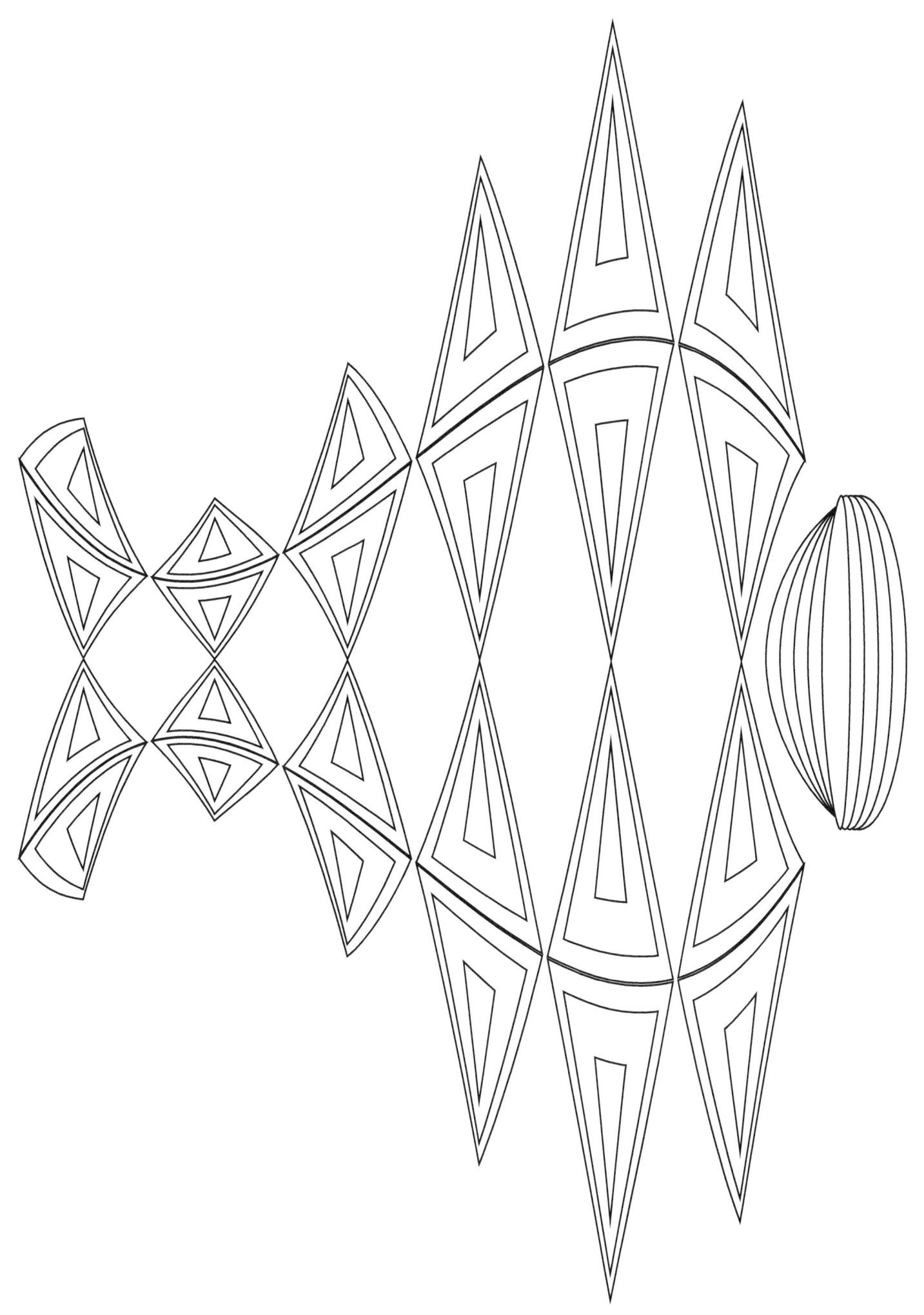

D# 1961

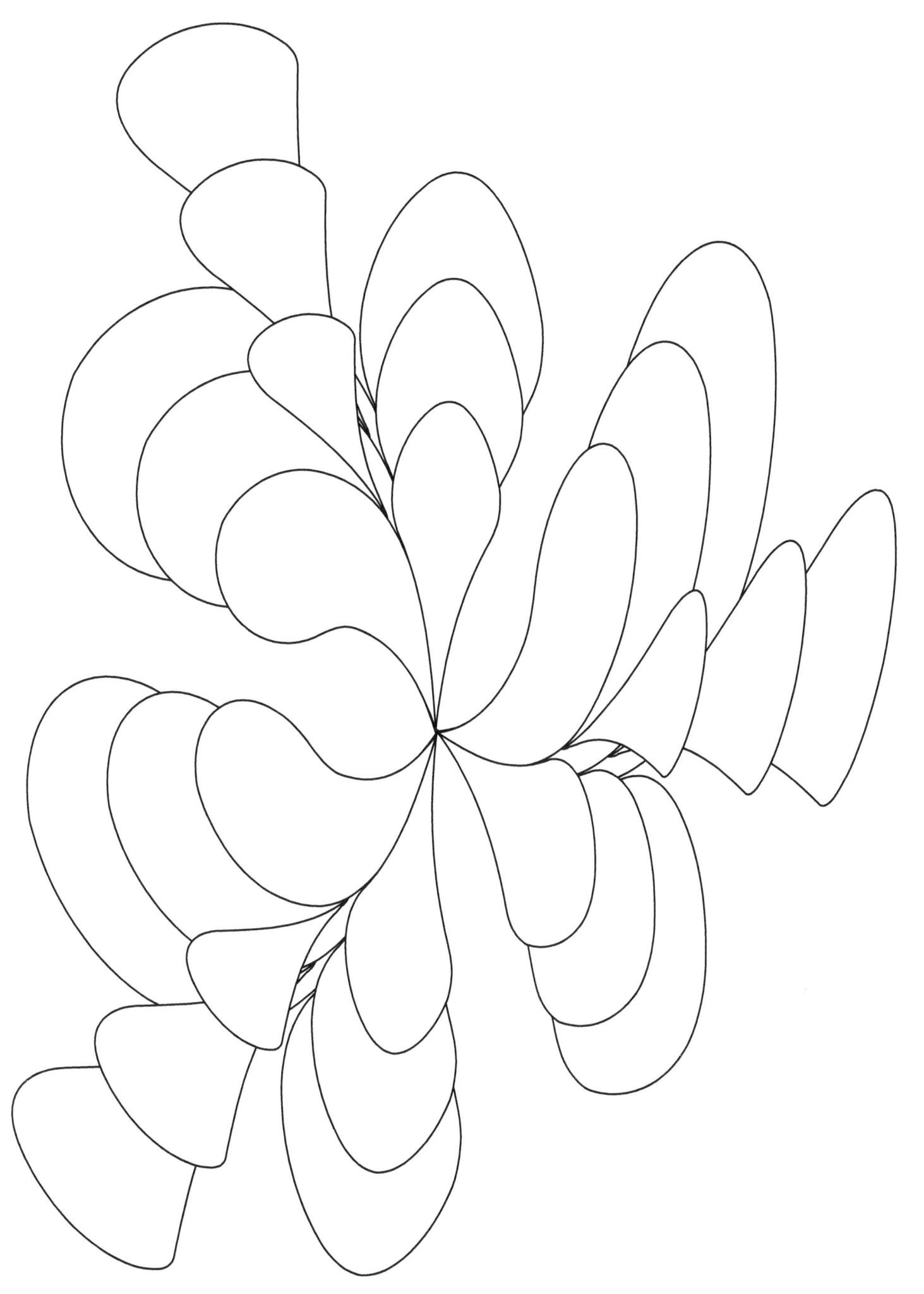

D# 1966

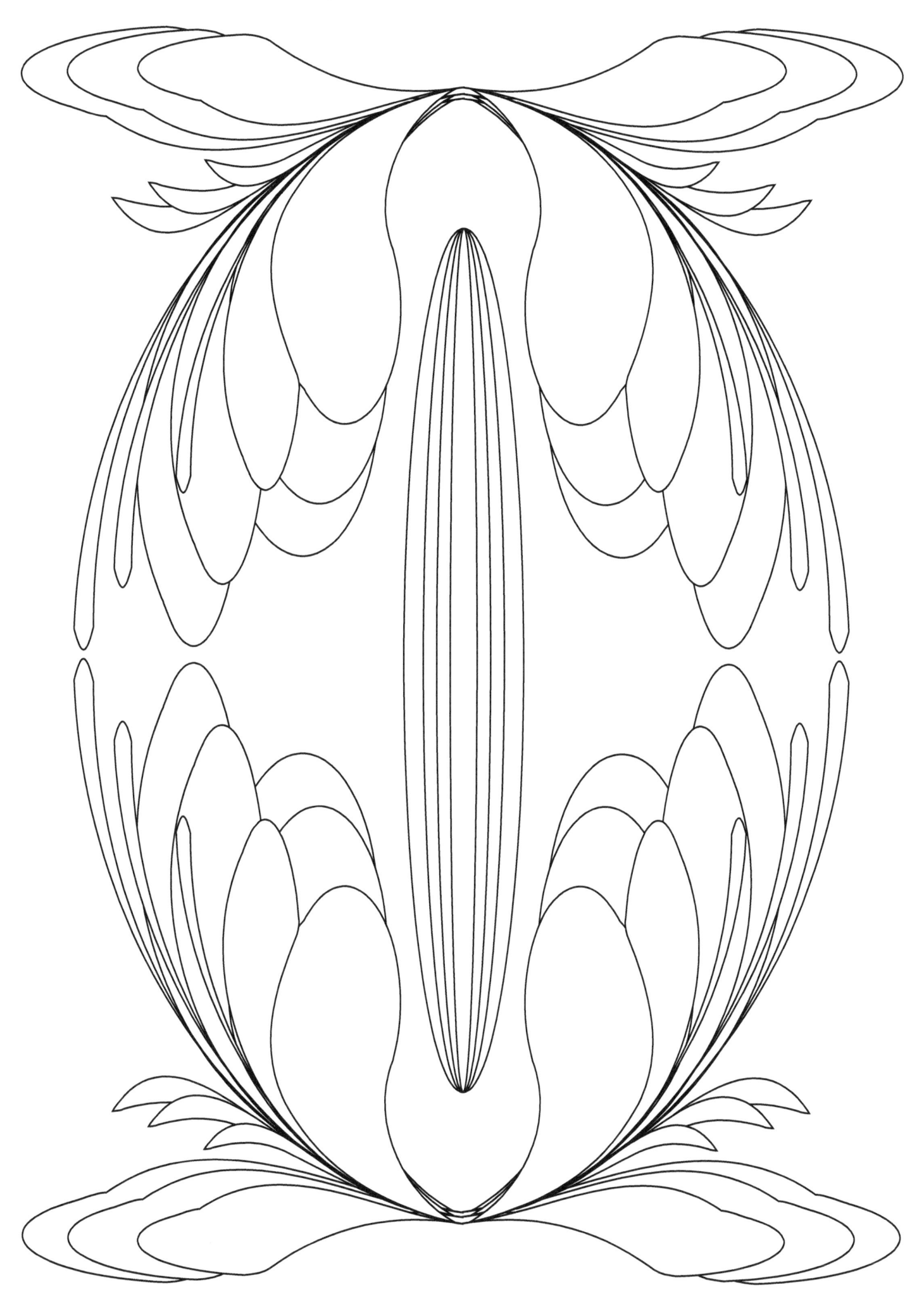

D# 1978

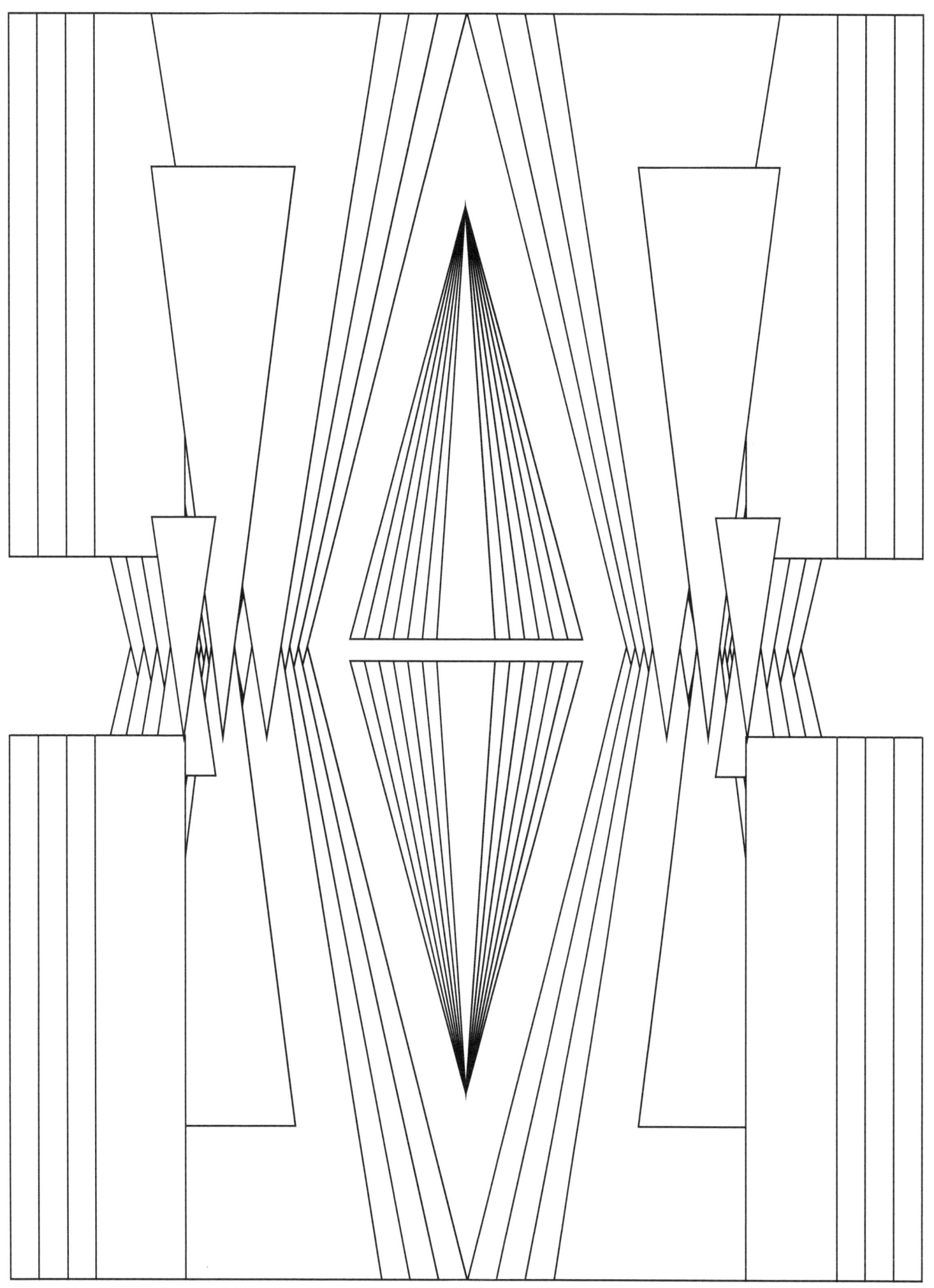

D# 2058

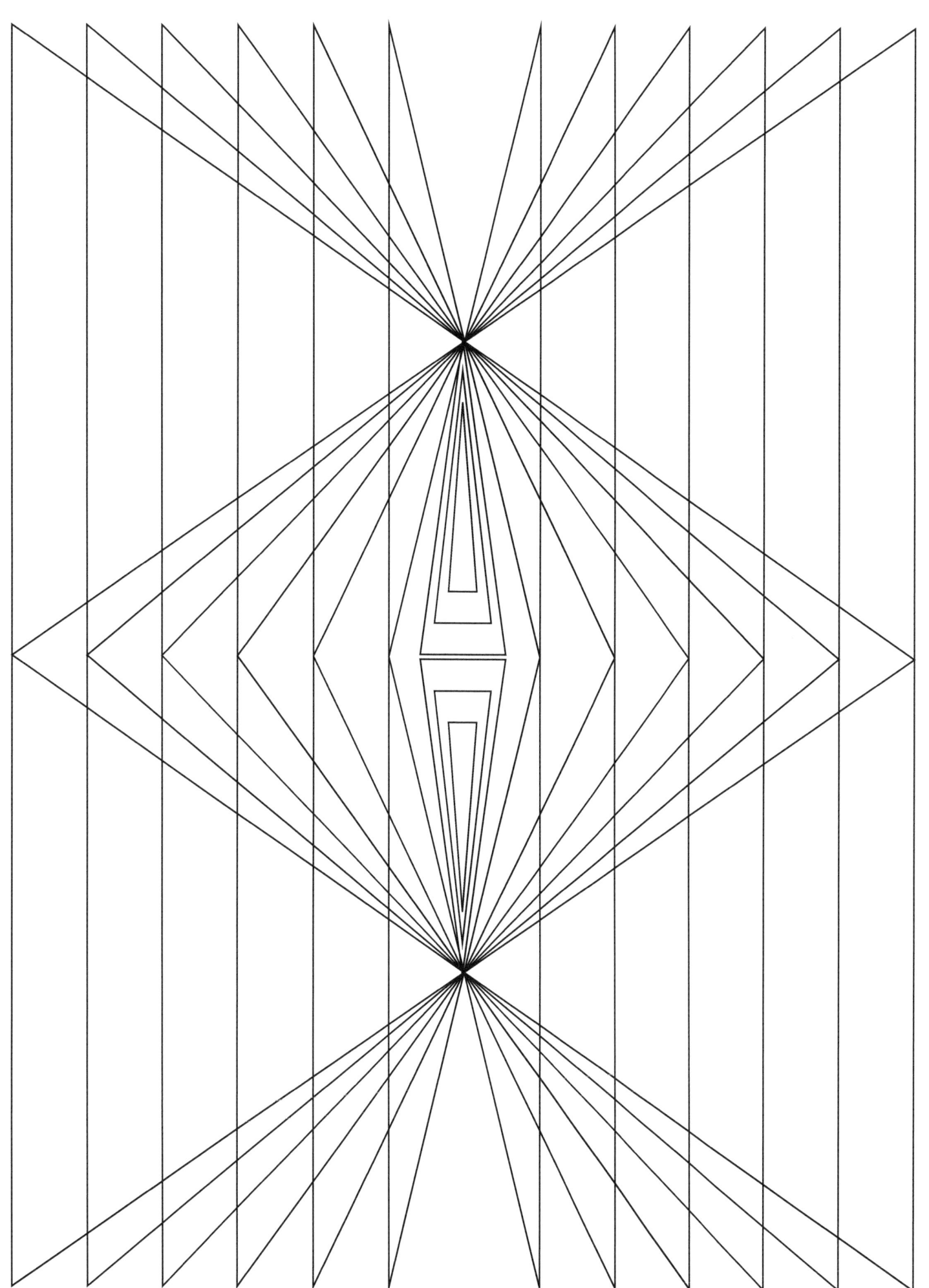

D# 2006

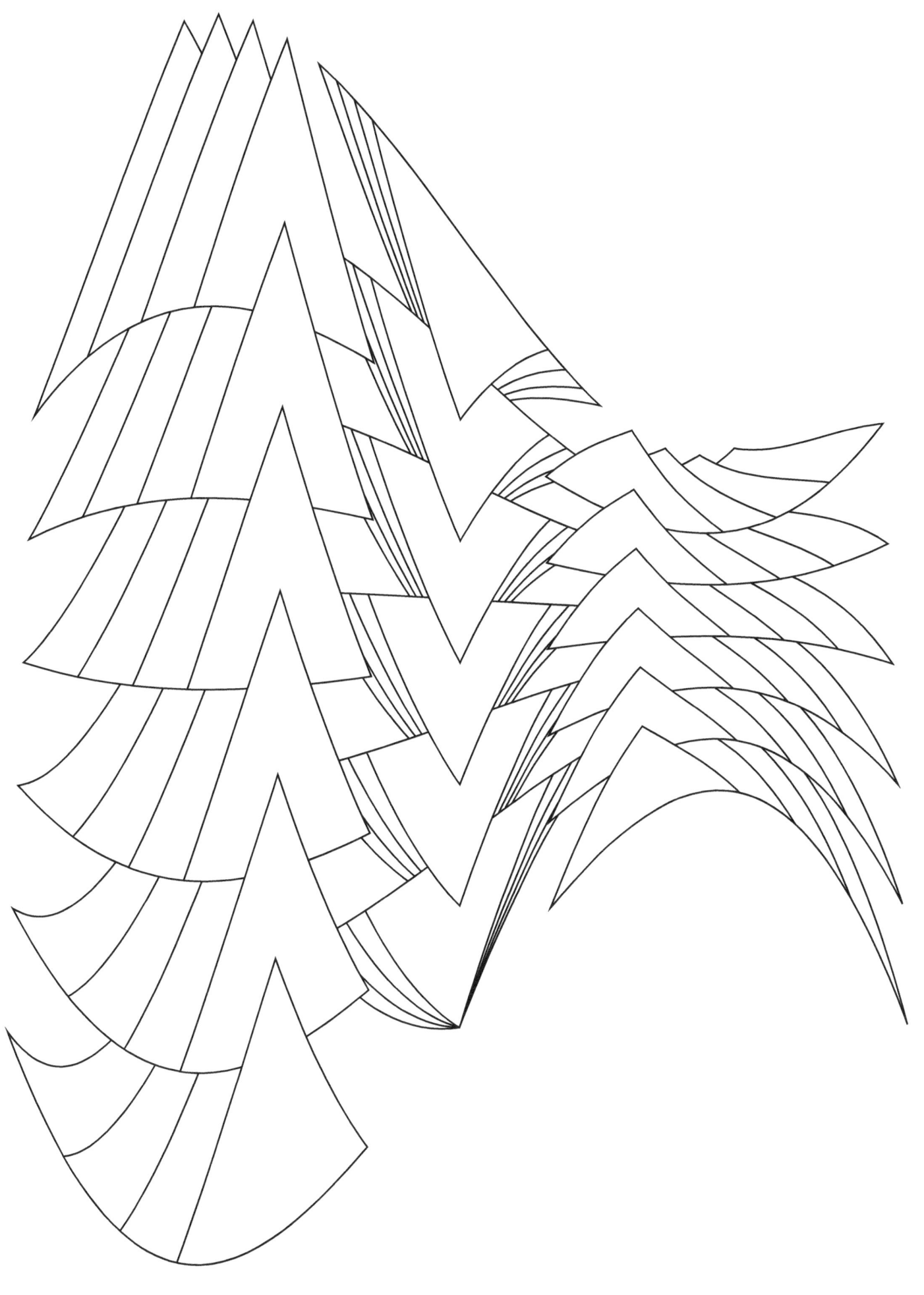

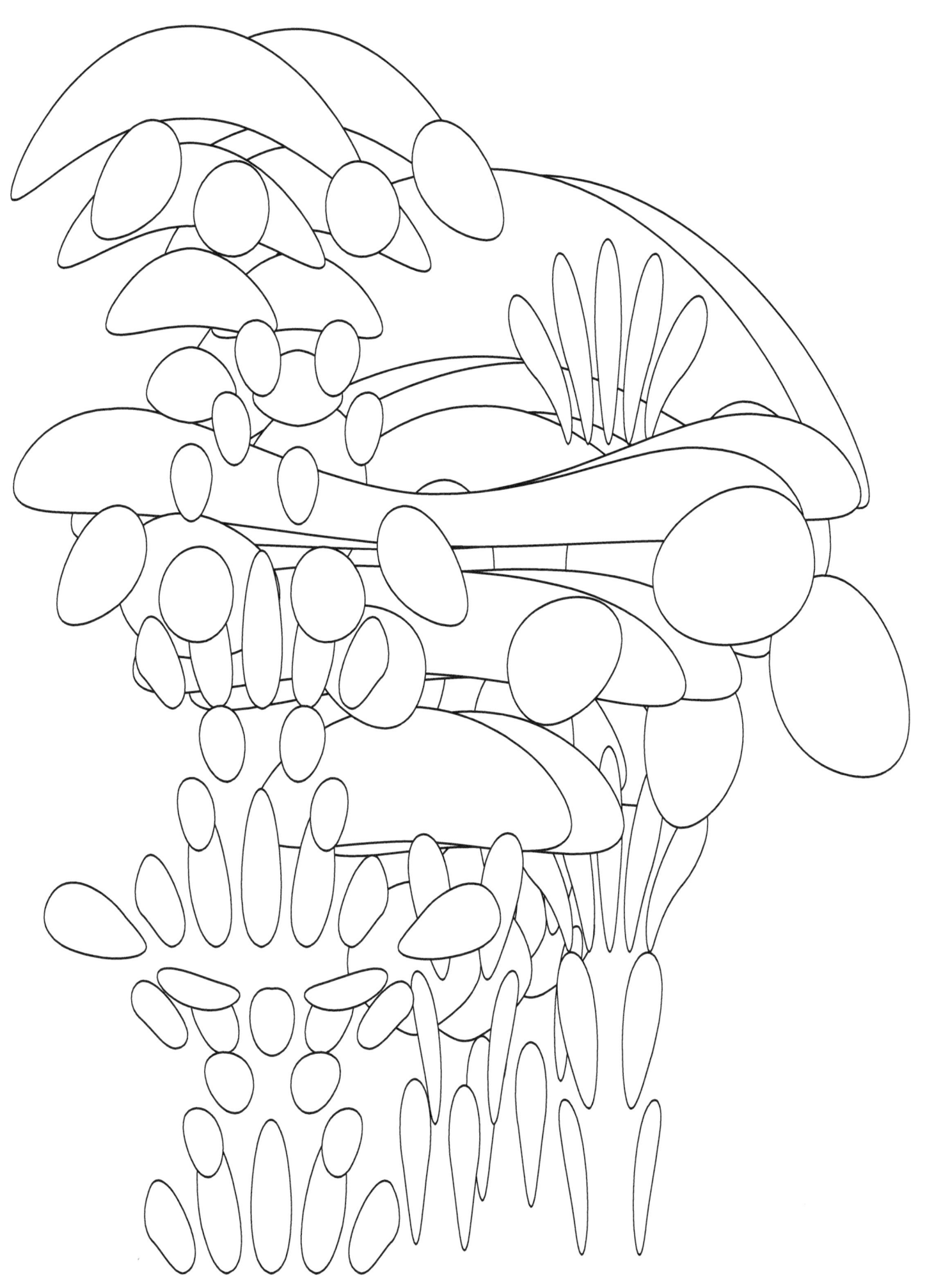

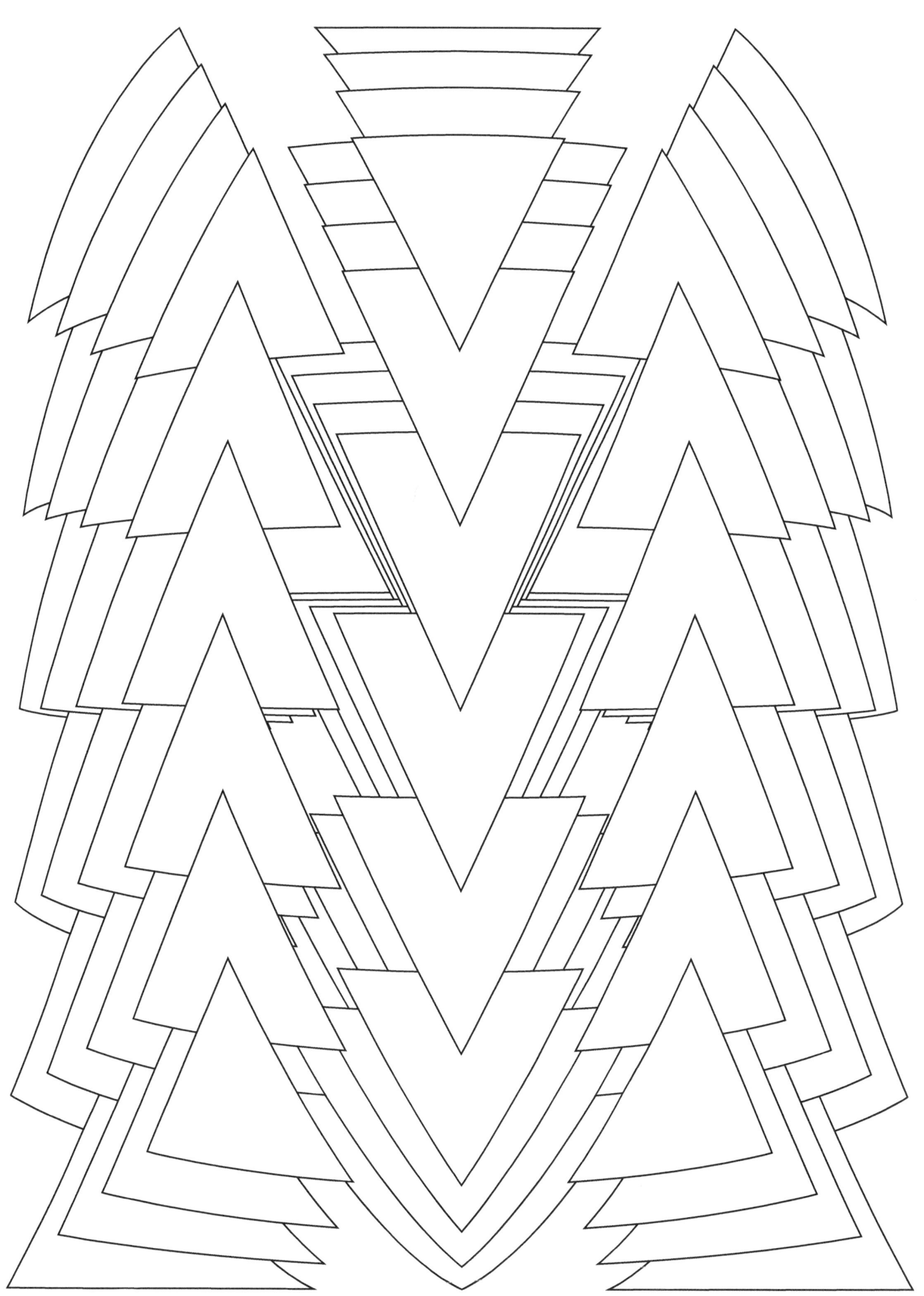

D# 2041

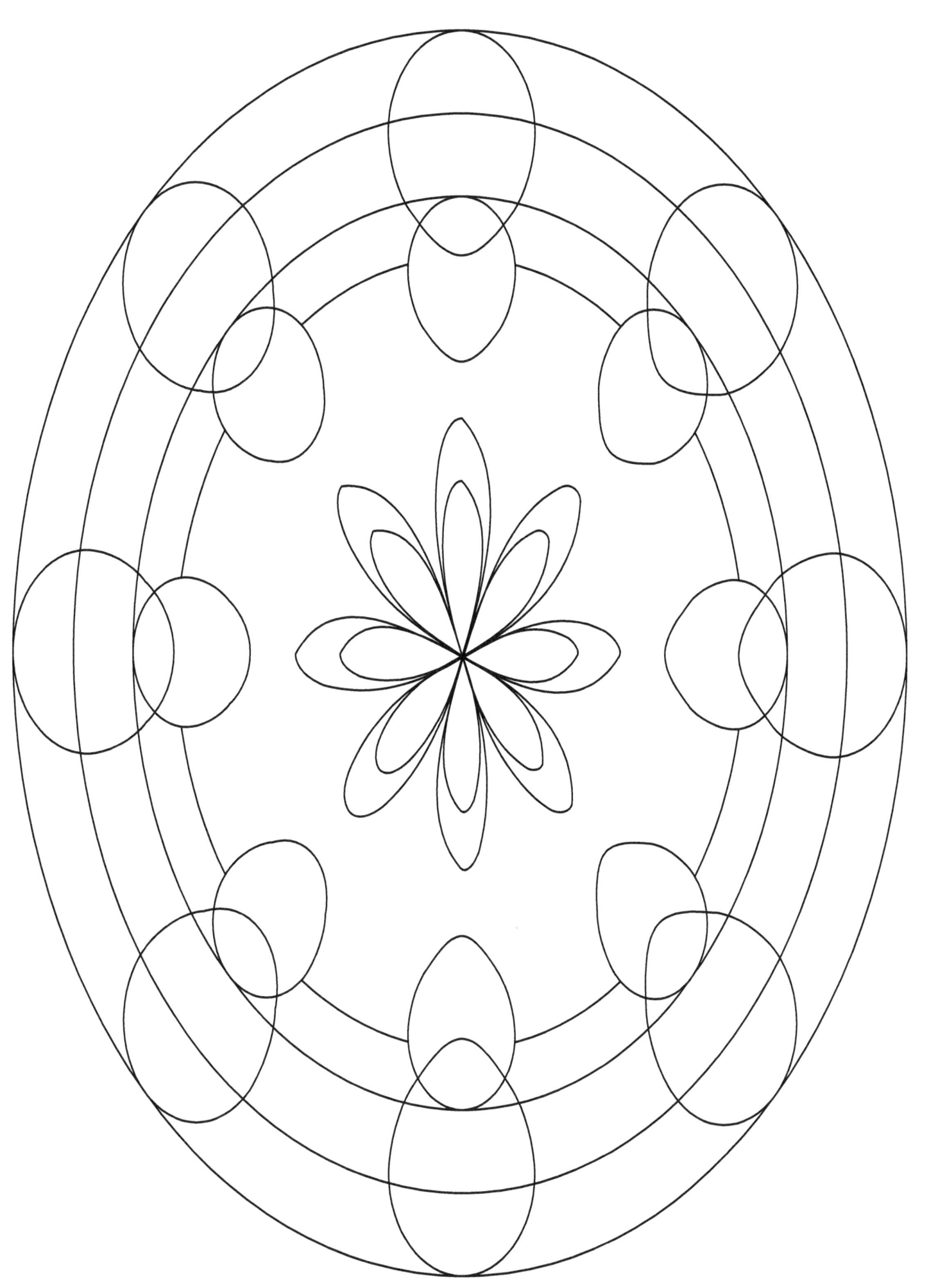

D# 2003

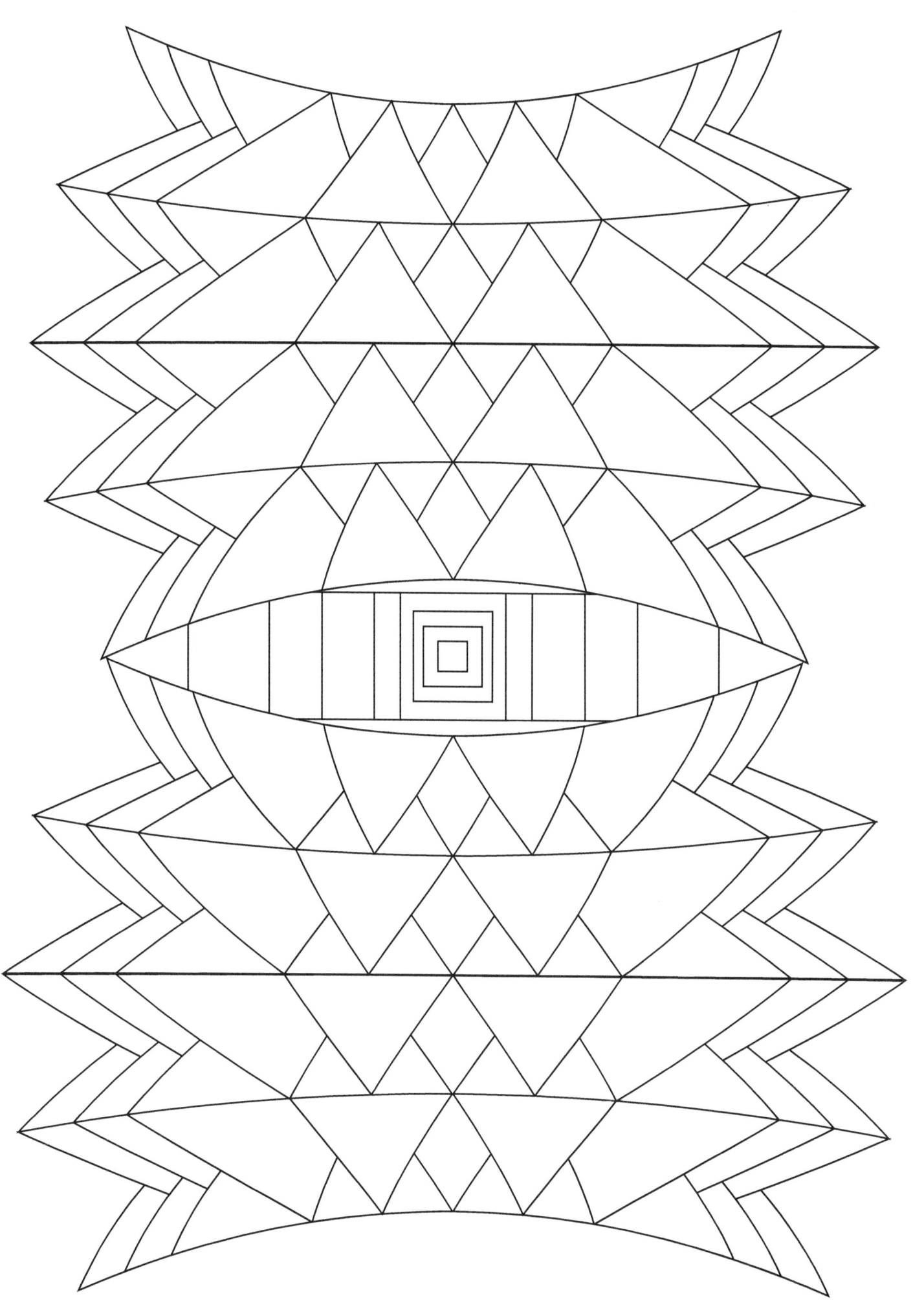

D# 2101

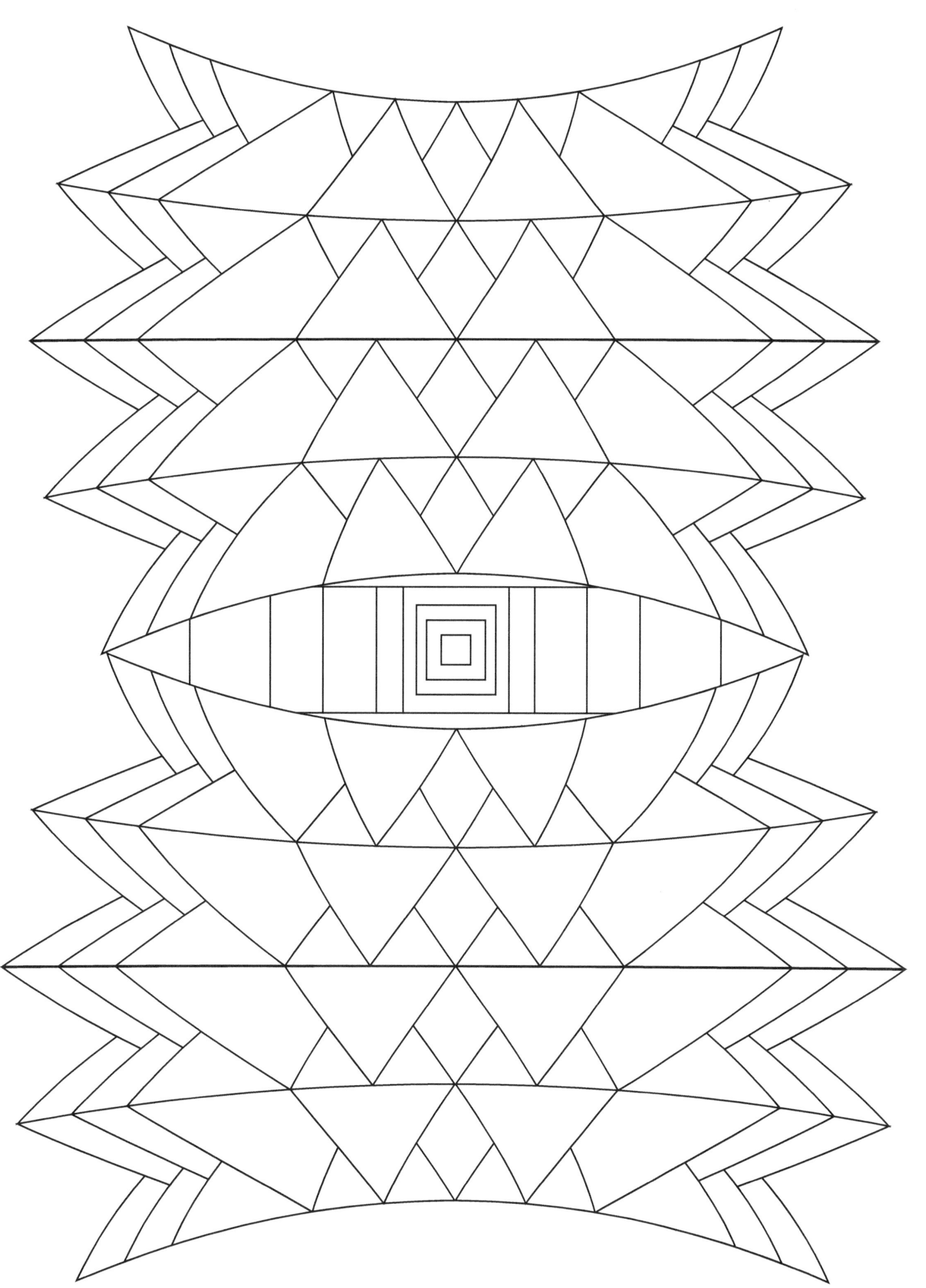

D# 2101

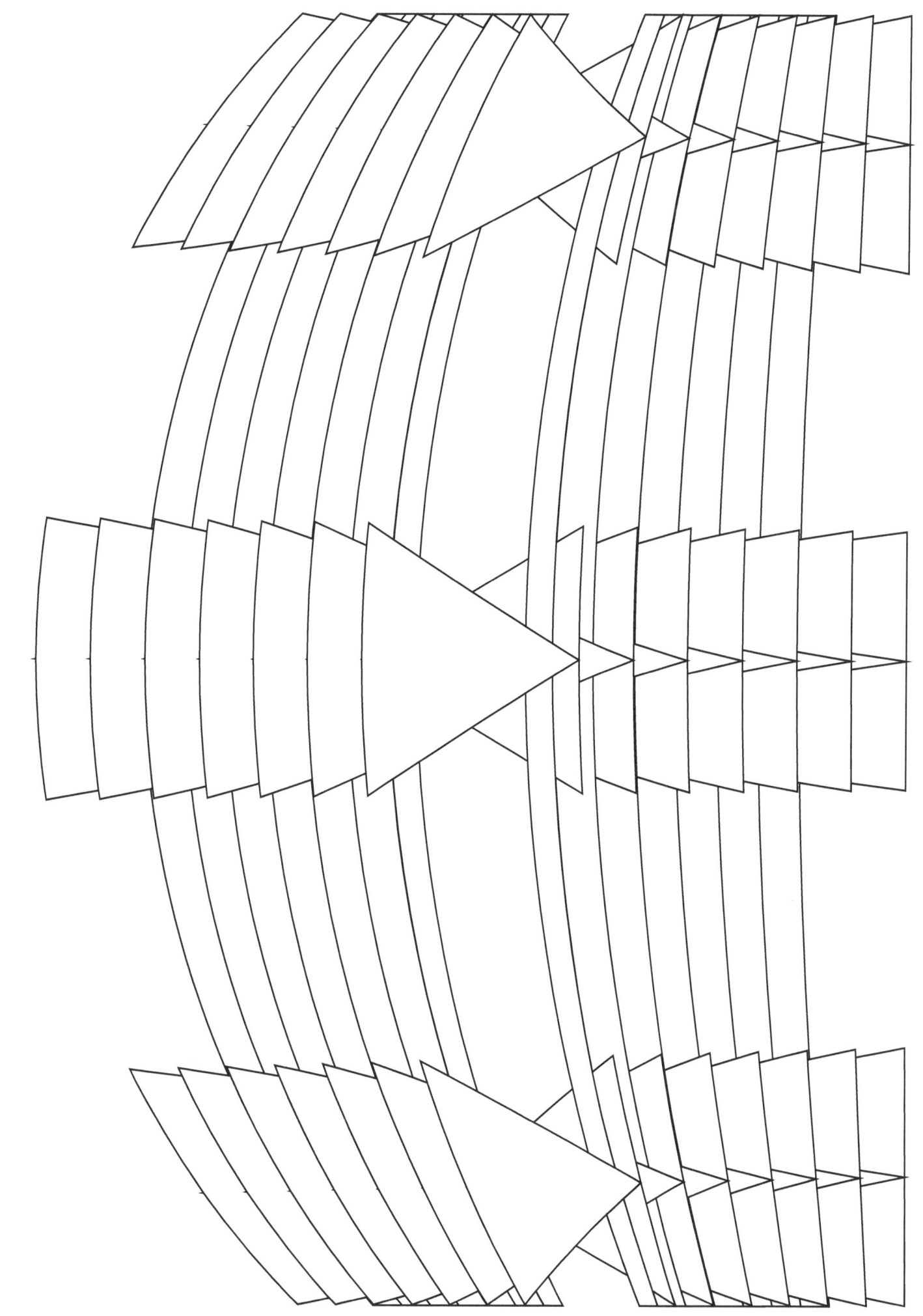